Introduction to
Law Enforcement

DANTES/DSST* Test Study Guide

All rights reserved. This Study Guide, Book and Flashcards are protected under the US Copyright Law. No part of this book or study guide or flashcards may be reproduced, distributed or stored in a retrieval system, or transmitted in any form or by any means, electronic, mechanical, photocopying, recording, or otherwise, without the prior written permission of the publisher Breely Crush Publishing, LLC.

© 2026 Breely Crush Publishing, LLC

*DSST is a registered trademark of The Thomson Corporation and its affiliated companies, and does not endorse this book.

971010620143

Copyright ©2003 - 2026, Breely Crush Publishing, LLC.

All rights reserved.

This Study Guide, Book and Flashcards are protected under the US Copyright Law. No part of this publication may be reproduced, distributed or stored in a retrieval system, or transmitted in any form or by any means, electronic, mechanical, photocopying, recording, or otherwise, without the prior written permission of the publisher Breely Crush Publishing, LLC.

Published by Breely Crush Publishing, LLC
10808 River Front Parkway
South Jordan, UT 84095
www.breelycrushpublishing.com

ISBN-10: 1-61433-674-1
ISBN-13: 978-1-61433-674-7

Printed and bound in the United States of America.

DSST is a registered trademark of The Thomson Corporation and its affiliated companies, and does not endorse this book.

Table of Contents

History and Professionalization of Law Enforcement 1
    Early American Policing 4
        Development of Modern Policing 5
        Early Corruption 6
        Important People in Policing History 7
        Racial Tension in Law Enforcement 8
Overview of the United States Criminal Justice System 9
    The Courts 9
        State Courts 9
        Federal Courts 10
    Police 11
    Corrections 11
        Prisons 12
        Community Corrections 13
        Criminal Justice Process 14
        Plea Bargaining 15
        Jury 16
        Trial 16
        Sentencing 17
        Measuring Crime 18
        NCVS 18
        UCR 19
        NIBRS 19
        Victimless Crime 20
Police Systems in the United States 20
    Federal Law Enforcement 20
        Homeland Security 20
        U.S. Marshals 21
        FBI 21
        Drug Enforcement Agency (DEA) 22
        Immigration and Customs Enforcement (ICE) 23
        State Law Enforcement Agencies 23
        Local Law Enforcement Agencies 24
        Sheriff's Departments 24
        City Police Departments 25
        Specialized Local law Enforcement 25
        Private Industry in Policing 25

- *Role of Police* *26*
  - *Enforce Laws* *26*
  - *Keeping the Peace* *27*
  - *Preventing Crimes* *28*
  - *Protecting Rights* *28*
  - *Providing Services* *29*
- *Police Organization* *30*
  - *Line staff/Field services* *30*
  - *Professionalization of Law Enforcement* *32*
    - *Training* *33*
    - *Accreditation* *33*
    - *Entrance Testing* *33*
    - *Educational Standards* *34*
    - *Promotional Standards* *34*
  - *Police Subculture* *35*
    - *Isolation* *35*
    - *Stress* *35*
    - *Secrecy in policing* *37*
  - *Police Deviance and Corruption* *37*
    - *The Lure of Corruption* *38*
    - *Combating corruption* *39*
    - *Internal Affairs* *40*
    - *Drug Testing of Employees* *40*
    - *Women and Minorities in Policing* *41*
    - *Police Discretion* *42*
  - *Policing Practices* *43*
    - *Styles of Policing* *43*
    - *Legalistic* *44*
    - *Watchman* *44*
    - *Service* *44*
    - *Police-Community Interaction* *44*
    - *Community Policing* *45*
- *Legal Aspects of Policing* *47*
  - *Warren Court* *48*
  - *Due Process* *48*
  - *Precedence* *49*
  - *Rules of Evidence* *49*
  - *Legalities Regarding Search and Seizure* *50*
    - *Additional exceptions* *53*
    - *Plain View* *53*

Vehicle Searches..*54*
    Emergency Exceptions..*55*
Legalities Regarding Arrests..*56*
    Search Incident to Arrest...*56*
    Emergency Searches of People..*57*
    Legalities Regarding Interrogation..*58*
Miranda Rights..*59*
    Waiving Miranda Rights..*60*
    Inevitable Discovery Exception...*60*
    Public Safety Exception...*60*
    Overview..*61*

Sample Test Questions..*62*
Test-Taking Strategies *93*
Test Preparation *94*
Legal Note *95*

 History and Professionalization of Law Enforcement

Law enforcement hasn't always been the organized structure we are now accustomed to seeing. From vigilante posses to regulated patrol, American police forces have undergone vast changes in the last few centuries. You cannot address modern day or even turn-of-the-century American policing without first examining its roots. Like much of our country's organizational structure, American law enforcement has been greatly influenced by Western Europe and particularly England.

Law enforcement had to begin with laws to enforce. One can assume that laws have been around for as long as man. However, finding proof of that is another story. One of the first written bodies of law still mostly intact is the Code of Hammurabi, instated by King Hammurabi of ancient Babylon. The Code is dated anywhere from 1700 to 2250 BC and contains common law violations and punishments to be meted out. This is where the commonly used term "eye for an eye" got its origins. *Lex talionis* was an early effort at establishing personal rights by proposing that one man's life is of no greater importance than another's, including even women and slaves. Also included in this early code of law were crimes, witchcraft, false accusations, taxes, loans, and debt. There were no religious references in the early law even though the black diorite stone it was etched on depicts King Hammurabi receiving the laws from the Babylonian God of Justice, Shamash. Archeologists discovered the Code of Hammurabi in modern day Iran and it is now housed in France.

The first record of people whose duty it was to enforce the laws goes back to ancient Egypt. Little information is available about these early police, but what has been determined through archaeological discoveries is that they carried a tool, similar to the batons used by police today, made of a large bat topped with a metal knob. Police ethics and brutality issues were not as worrisome as they are today.

A sort of cross between judge and police were the Greek **ephor**, used as early as the 8th Century B.C. The five ephori made up a panel of men who oversaw everything from civil resolutions to enforcement of the King's rule. These men were elected to their position and every citizen was entitled to run. However, the ephori were a small elite group that was plagued by corruption. One unique power of the ephor was to arrest the King if necessary.

Law evolved through time, eventually finding itself in Rome where advances were made as the law was first separated into two distinct divisions, private and public laws, similar to modern day civil and criminal law. The Emperor Augustus further developed the role and organization of law enforcement with two bodies of police. The first was an elite team of soldiers from his army. These soldiers were tasked with guarding the palace and patrolling Rome. Also, a group of firefighters took on law enforcement roles. This group was called the ***vigiles urbani***. The vigiles patrolled the city, particularly in the evening, looking for fires and law violators. In the mid-second century, the vigiles began working out of command posts made specifically for their use. These could be considered the first police departments. Interestingly, modern day police forces in Italy are often still referred to as the *vigiles urbani*, or "watchmen of the city."

Another group in Ancient Rome also had law enforcement powers. **Lictors** were officers of the court tasked with protecting the magistrates, among other things. They would arrest and detain criminals, bringing them before the magistrate. Often, lictors were required to actually carry out an execution at the request of their magistrate. The lictors carried a long staff with an ax attached to it. These **fasces** were mostly a symbol of power.

Evolution of law in England led to the feudal system. The feudal system was one founded on community governing and was dominant from the 9th to the 14th centuries. It was a hierarchal system based off the land. The lord of the land ruled over his vassals and then over his servants. Disputes between any of the latter were taken up with the lord who acted as a judge over his land. This mediation practice seemed to work well for the time.

Following the feudal system in England was the **tithing system**. The tithing system allowed members of the community to govern themselves by forming organized associations of cooperating families. These groups, or **tithes**, were each made up of ten families. One man would represent each family in the tithe and would assist with the law enforcement and conflict resolution within the group. One member of the tithe would be in charge and referred to as the ***chief* tithingman**. This administrative figure would serve in a capacity similar to that of a mayor.

Laws of the tithe and the country were enforced by community governing. If one person in the tithe committed a crime and was convicted, the entire group would be responsible for the imposed fine. The hope was that by imposing potential punishments on the entire group, the tithe would be accountable for each other and work to be law abiding citizens.

The tithing system established simple solutions to crime. At that time, crime was fairly cut and dried. The people were looking to prevent murder and theft. This community-based policing allowed every member of the tithing to get involved in crime prevention.

The **hue and cry** method required that if a citizen saw a law be violated they would shout to call attention to it and to stop the criminal. By "crying" out to the community that a theft, or murder, had taken place, the citizens within earshot were required to stop what they were doing and assist in the apprehension. This was the predecessor to the modern day citizen's arrest. The apprehended criminal would face the chief tithingman for determination of guilt and meting out of punishment. Popular punishments of the time were fines, restitution, or working off the debt through servitude.

Reeve was the term used to refer to a group of ten tithes. A group of reeves formed a **shire**. Each shire also had a chief who was called the **shire-reeve**. The shire-reeve was considered the head judge and police officer and would travel from reeve to reeve within his shire carrying out his duties of punishment and enforcement. The modern day term *sheriff* is derived from the "shire-reeve."

One unique power of the shire-reeve was his ability to gather many men together to pursue a criminal. This group was the *posse comitatus*, and was the predecessor to the posses in the wild West. In Latin, *posse comitatus* refers to the *power of the land*.

Another modern day concept that originated in this era was extradition. If a fleeing criminal was found in another tithe, the chief tithingman or members of that tithe were required to return the suspect to the tithe of origination to face his punishment.

England was invaded by the Normans, led by William the Conqueror, in 1066. He brought with him the Frankpledge system and seriously changed the existing system of tithes. First, he changed the role of the shire-reeve by making it solely one of law enforcement. Each shire-reeve's territory included a military district. The shire-reeves answered directly to the King. He then appointed judges to travel the countryside ruling on disputes and law violations. This marked the first clear separation of courts and law enforcement.

The **Frankpledge** system expanded on the existing community system. It required that all men pledge peace to the King. This meant that all men agreed to do whatever possible to keep the peace for the sake of the throne. This did not change the basis of the tithing system, community accountability, but merely added the King as another party to it.

William the Conqueror also brought with him new laws including curfews, tax laws, and written documentation appropriating punishments for particular crimes.

The son of William the Conqueror, King Henry I ruled from 1068-1135. He, like his father, helped law enforcement and the justice system evolve even further. He implemented the **Leges Henrici** establishing that certain crimes that were inherently bad, should not only be considered crimes against the community, but crimes against the throne. This established that some crimes needed to, therefore, be punished by the government as well. These laws included murder, arson, and robbery among others. This further move toward institutionalization of law enforcement laid the groundwork for government-run policing agencies.

The population boomed and so did crime. It became apparent that community members were either not holding up their end of the bargain, or were not able to. In the 1600s, **constables** began patrolling the streets actively looking for petty criminals and attempting to prevent crime. This early organizational system was a start, but didn't have the numbers or professionalism needed to rein in crime.

In an effort to encourage community involvement, in the late 17th century the English government started offering substantial rewards for the apprehension of criminals. From this evolved a group of individuals called **thief takers**. Thief takers did exactly what their name implied; they captured criminals and returned stolen goods to victims of theft who offered the right reward. Often, these thief takers were crooks themselves, orchestrating schemes to make money from both the thieves themselves and the victims they preyed upon. Because the rewards offered didn't require anyone specific to respond, they allowed everyone in general to become law enforcement. The thief takers were often petty criminals themselves, looking to capitalize on the misfortune of others.

Exposure to the criminal underground allowed them to serve both sides of the conflict. In the early 1700s, stations were set up around London where citizens could find a magistrate when needed. One of these stations was located on Bow Street. Magistrates and brothers Henry and John Fielding worked out of the Bow Street station and employed more favorable thief takers as "runners." These runners, later known as the **Bow Street Runners**, would be sent out of the station when a crime was reported to apprehend the suspect. By centralizing a group of thief takers, the Fieldings hoped to improve the reputation and activities of the local law enforcement. The implementation of the Bow Street Runners marked a move toward real professionalization of the police force.

Modern day policing can be directly traced to the creation of the **London Metropolitan Police Force** in 1829 by Sir Robert Peel. Legendary in nature, this police force was a true professional agency. The first of its kind, it employed upstanding men and provided them with uniforms and training. Reception of the new police wasn't very warm. The proactive policing employed by the "bobbies," as they became known, was initially a nuisance to the crime-ridden neighborhoods they frequented. Once their practices became common, however, law abiding citizens rallied behind them.

EARLY AMERICAN POLICING

Similar to early English police, Americans tried many methods to keep the peace. Because it was a new country that put an emphasis on state and local control over such things, there was little uniformity from colony to colony and later from state to state.

Establishing night watches and guards was one of the early methods utilized in colonial America. New immigrants, who made up the country, wanted their homes and families protected from criminals with little interference from the government. By first drafting citizens for the night watch and later paying the men, they hoped to avoid government influence in local law enforcement. This night watch system was the primary means of law enforcement in the northern colonies and later states.

A sort of posse comitatus of **slave patrols** ruled in the South. These patrols, with the primary purpose of stopping, punishing, and returning runaway slaves, was considered one of the more modern, albeit archaic, police forces in early America. Charleston, South Carolina had an active slave patrol of over 100 men in 1837 and at the time was the largest "police force."

Out West the Sheriff's role was developed, modeled after the English *shire reeve*. The sheriff was the law of the land and could appoint deputies as he saw fit. The West was truly wild back then and provided a breeding ground for criminals and thieves. Sheriffs were often volunteers not compensated for their work.

DEVELOPMENT OF MODERN POLICING

In 1631 the city of Boston organized a group of six men to serve as the city guard. They would serve from sundown to sunup as the first organized night watchmen group in the United States. This system stayed in effect in Boston for over 200 years. Their duties, however, changed and grew over time. Beginning in 1801 the force was paid and each man received fifty cents per night of work. In 1838 a day force was created to assist with the duties of the night watch. The police force in Boston was one of the earliest *modern* forces in the new world.

In New York, settled by the Dutch and originally called New Amsterdam, the **sheriff attorney** was the first in law enforcement. This position, created in 1624, encompassed police and prosecutor. The sheriff attorney was tasked with enforcing the laws of the Dutch West India Company. Law enforcement quickly evolved in the city and a **burgher guard** was created in 1643 to protect the colony. This position quickly changed to a **rattle watch**. The rattle watch patrolled at night and carried with them rattles to call for help. In 1658 the rattle watch was replaced by six men (in a city of now 800) who would serve as night watchmen; these six men were considered the first police in New York.

In 1664, after the English took over and changed the city name to New York, a uniformed force also moved in. Around this time the streets of New York became lighted as well. Prior to this the streets were dark aside from personal lanterns. The lighting of the streets helped quell crime that was taking place under the cover of darkness.

The early systems were very ineffective. With no training and often no pay, the men who served as watchmen did not have much interest in the work they were doing. A common punishment for petty crimes in the day was to force the offenders to serve as night watchmen. Not only did this mean that criminals were protecting the streets at night but also that night watch duty was considered tedious and unimportant. Another reason for corruption and ineffectiveness was that someone could get out of watch duty by paying someone else to do it. This lack of accountability was another indication that the position was not one of professionalism or true concern.

Further perpetuating the less than professional force was the new day watch in New York City. The city decided a group of watchmen was needed in the daylight hours to assist with crime prevention as well. This group of men was kept entirely separate from the night watch and serious animosity developed between those watchmen who worked during the daylight hours and those who guarded the city at night.

In 1844, after visiting the London Metropolitan Police Force, administrators decided to model Robert Peel's design in New York. That year New York City developed the first *modern* American police force. The officers were trained, paid, and uniformed. Recognizing the value of a professional force and following suit quite readily were cities like San Francisco, Boston, Baltimore, and Chicago. The first detective bureau began in 1882 in Chicago.

EARLY CORRUPTION

Corruption in early departments was rampant. Law enforcement had been a mixed group of petty criminals and regular citizens. Weeding out those who still had a negative mindset continued indefinitely. One of the primary concerns of police corruption was the **spoils system**, which stated "to the victor go the spoils." What this meant was those who were powerful in the community believed their people or friends should not be held accountable to the law. They felt that they, and those associated with them, were above the law because of their power. With no one to argue otherwise, police departments were often riddled with friends and family members of powerful people, getting away with just about everything.

This political influence on law enforcement was exactly what colonial Americans were trying to avoid. Communities did not want those who were supposed to be protecting them, actually causing more harm than good. Reform efforts were slow in coming because of the power of the elite few. By setting up boards and asking state government for assistance, local agencies slowly moved toward a more ethical system.

One creation spawned by reform movements was the post of **police chief**. This elected official became the head of departments across the nation. By making this post elected rather than appointed, the people hoped to eliminate the spoils system. However, in an effort to reduce corruption the terms were very short. So short, in fact, that before a chief could make any difference, his term would be up. Early police chiefs would keep their previous jobs, knowing they wouldn't be chief for long. This meant that the law enforcement role would often take a back seat to the individual's regular job.

Further tweaking the system was the development of administrative boards. These boards were made up of judges, citizens and mayors in an effort to oversee the Chiefs of Police. The line of thought was that terms could be extended to encourage further development of the post as long as the post was being overseen by an impartial board. Again, this system was not out of reach of the long arm of corruption and although they lasted many years, the administrative police boards were not the right fit.

Following the administrative police boards in the trial and error of early law enforcement, was the commission government charter. Unfortunately commissioners proved to be no better than the boards and the system quickly died off as well.

In 1883, the **Pendleton Act** was passed by Congress in an attempt to reduce corruption. This important Act created the civil service system. It made it illegal to fire someone for political reasons and created the testing process that is used in hiring law enforcement even today. Assuring only the best candidates made it into law enforcement, regardless of their connections, it created a force that promised to be the least corrupt thus far.

IMPORTANT PEOPLE IN POLICING HISTORY

Important in the professionalization of early American law enforcement was **August Vollmer**. Using his military experience and studies of criminal justice, Vollmer reinvented the Berkley California Police Department where he served as Chief beginning in 1909. Later known as the "father of modern law enforcement," Vollmer created a bicycle patrol and a motorcycle patrol. He is credited with developing the first centralized police records system. He also was the first to require all police officers have a college degree. Developing a criminal justice program at the University of California, Vollmer attempted to make the field a well known and well respected aspect of academia.

Taught by August Vollmer in that esteemed criminal justice program at the University of California was **Orlando Wilson**. Graduating from the University, Wilson went on to serve under Vollmer in the Berkley Police Department. He later served as Chief of Police in Wichita. His most well known accomplishment, however, was serving as the Superintendant of Police in the city of Chicago beginning in 1960. Wilson was responsible for streamlining hiring and training practices within the Chicago department as well as bringing technology to the force. Computers were used in the force and patrol cars were plenty. The Chicago police department garnered respect from the people they served.

RACIAL TENSION IN LAW ENFORCEMENT

The 1960s marked a time in United States history of civil unrest. From race riots to anti-war protests, the police were involved in many explosive situations. These situations brought to light even more issues with law enforcement and their abuses of power. It was during this time that racism in law enforcement was beginning to be investigated. All-white forces were very common and little was done to diversify them both in appearance and attitude. Many riots were blamed on the police. The police were often seen as perpetuators of turmoil rather than keepers of peace.

The **Kerner Commission**, developed under President Lyndon B. Johnson, **addressed** issues such as police brutality, riots, and discrimination. It held that largely due to law enforcement, a wedge was increasing the racial divide in America. It was the Kerner Commission who warned that we were moving toward a country that was "separate but unequal." This brought racial issues and tension to the forefront in law enforcement.

Guidelines were implemented concerning uses of force to address racial disparities. Affirmative action policies were put into practice for hiring of officers. The police began meeting with members of the minority community. All of this was done in an effort to create a bridge from the powerful arm of the law to the minority people it should have been providing equal protection to the entire time.

In the late 1970s, 1980s, and 1990s, crime rates skyrocketed. All types of crimes were at all time highs. Drugs were rampant and largely causing an increase in crime across the board. Crime control once again became a major priority and police scrambled to make a difference in the climbing rates. This is where the "tough on crime" era began. By arresting offenders and giving harsh sentences, the entire criminal justice system sought to deter crime. Commonly held beliefs were that neighborhood watches and good intentions were not effective enough and that high volume patrols in troubled neighborhoods and bringing the "heat" onto repeat offenders were effective methods of reducing crime.

 Overview of the United States Criminal Justice System

The United States criminal justice system is vast. It is separated into three branches: courts, law enforcement, and corrections.

THE COURTS

The role of the courts in the United States criminal justice system is to interpret and apply the laws. Courts in this country are either Federal or State. Because the founding fathers wanted to keep big government limited, the state systems were created as a means of governing locally.

STATE COURTS

Each state differs in the organization of their courts. The majority of states, however, modeled their systems after the federal courts. Some states have remained separate from the federal system and are resistant to change. A move toward uniformity among states has been a long-standing and difficult one. The adoption of similar systems across the country would make for simplification and streamlined processing

Those states that mimic the federal model have a three-tiered system. Those three tiers include:

1. Trial courts with limited jurisdiction (lower courts)
2. Trial courts with general jurisdiction (higher courts)
3. Appellate courts

Even though states may model their system after the federal courts, there are always slight differences. Most states have smaller more specialized courts in addition to these listed. Drug courts and traffic courts are just a few examples.

Courts of **limited jurisdiction** refer to those who can only hear certain aspects of certain cases. This may be the only stop for misdemeanors and they may not hear felonies at all. However, courts of **general jurisdiction** are those that can hear all cases, regardless of class or severity.

More often than not, states have two types of appellate courts. At the base are regular courts of appeals, which most states have. However, all states have a state supreme court, which is included under this heading of "appellate" courts. An appeals court does not hold an additional trial but merely reviews the trial that happened in the lower courts. If the court of appeals finds reason to overturn the original ruling, that case may be sent back to a court of limited jurisdiction for a new trial.

If either side of the case is not happy with the decision of the appellate court, it can be appealed for further review to the state supreme court. Again, if either party is not happy with what the state Supreme Court finds, the case can then be appealed to the United States Supreme Court.

FEDERAL COURTS

The Federal court system also has three tiers:

1. U.S. District Courts
2. U.S. Courts of Appeals
3. U.S. Supreme Court

There are currently 94 district courts within the U.S. court system. Every state has at least one federal district court, and some have more. There are also federal courts in Puerto Rico, Guam, the District of Columbia, the Virgin Islands, and the Northern Marina Islands. These courts are the courts of **original jurisdiction** for all federal offenses. This simply means that every federal case will start in the federal district court. The majority of them will end here as well.

Federal district court judges are appointed by the president and serve life terms. Multiple judges sit in each district court. Federal magistrates are appointed by the District judges and only serve eight-year terms. The types of cases that magistrates hear are dictated by statute and vary from state to state. The district court judge with the most seniority typically holds the position of Chief and performs administrative duties.

A group of federal districts create a **circuit**. There are 13 circuits in the United States, each with a U.S. Court of Appeals. These courts hear cases on appeal from the United States District Courts. The circuit court judges, like the district court judges, are appointed by the president, confirmed by the senate, and serve a life term.

These circuit courts have *mandatory* jurisdiction over the cases that are brought to them. This means that every case brought to the U.S. Circuit courts on appeal, must be reviewed. Cases are typically reviewed by a panel of three judges.

The highest court of the nation, the **United States Supreme Court** is seated in our nation's capital and is made up of nine justices. The Supreme Court Justices are, like all other federal judges, appointed by the president and confirmed by the senate to serve a lifelong term on the bench. One justice serves as the Chief Justice and serves in this position for the life of his term.

The Supreme Court has a power called **judicial review**. This means that the Supreme Court can review any case from any court in the nation. Also a unique characteristic of the Supreme Court is that it possesses **appellate jurisdiction**. Unlike circuit courts, the United States Supreme Court gets to choose which cases it wants to review from the thousands sent to it every year. The Supreme Court only chooses cases whose evaluation may alter or uphold prior constitutional evaluations.

POLICE

The major role of police in the United States is to enforce the law. The police are the muscle of the criminal justice system. It is their duty to be on the streets stopping crime before it happens and apprehending people after a crime has occurred. Police powers are granted through state and federal statute.

Although the main purpose of the police is to enforce the laws, over time that role has been greatly expanded to include such duties as:

1. Enforce laws
2. Keep the peace
3. Prevent Crimes
4. Protect Rights
5. Provide Services

While every law enforcement agency has its own unique and particular purposes and goals, the above lists those that are most common across the board. Qualities and policies unique to law enforcement are addressed throughout this text.

CORRECTIONS

The branch of Corrections serves to carry out and enforce criminal sentences from the courts. It encompasses jails, prisons, as well as community sanctions such as probation and halfway houses. There are four goals of corrections that are important to address:

1. Deterrence
2. Rehabilitation
3. Retribution
4. Incapacitation

Each of these goals represents one theory or method of applying corrections. Throughout history corrections has at one time or another practiced all four of these goals, whether using them exclusively or in conjunction with one another.

Deterrence refers to preventing future crime from being committed. When a sentence prevents the specific defendant from committing another offense it is called **specific deterrence**. However, when a sentence is imposed to have the defendant serve as an example in hopes that it will prevent *other* individuals from committing future offenses, it is referred to as **general deterrence**.

Rehabilitation is the goal that focuses on changing the offender through sentencing. Corrections first started using rehabilitative facets in the 1930s and since then the rehabilitative aspect of corrections has grown tremendously. Rehabilitative corrections focus on such things as mental health therapies, drug and alcohol treatments and a relearning of some of life's basic lessons. This goal is founded on the principal that most everyone is capable of change and poor decision making skills can be relearned to change criminals into productive members of society.

Retribution is an old goal of corrections and an ancient goal of criminal justice as a whole. This goal goes back to *lex talionis* or the "eye for an eye" principal. Retribution states the criminals need to pay for their actions and sees corrections as solely a system of punishment. Often criticized for being archaic and not progressive, retribution is still at the forefront when society decides to take a "tough on crime" stance.

Incapacitation as a goal means removing the offender's ability to commit a crime. Prison is the most common form of incapacitation. When criminals are locked away they cannot commit crimes (at least in the general public). Chemical castration is also an extreme example of incapacitation. Similar to cutting off the hands of a thief, chemical castration seeks to stop the criminal act by removing the means by which to commit it. The most extreme form of incapacitation, of course, would be the death penalty.

PRISONS

In early America there were no prisons. Jails existed to house local offenders. The first American prisons, however, were not constructed until the early 1800s. Two schools of penitentiary methodology arose at this time: the Auburn system and the Pennsylvania system.

The **Auburn system** arose in New York at Auburn State Prison. The inmates there were subjected to hard labor every day, all day long. They were not allowed to speak, at all. They returned to their single-man cells at night only to return to the same pattern the next day. It was thought that this hard work and silence would deter criminals while allowing prisons to pay for themselves. The Auburn system began a corrupt system of slave labor in American prisons.

The **Pennsylvania system** took a completely different approach by requiring absolute solitude from the inmates in Cherry Hill, Pennsylvania. The inmates here were confined to their single-man cells all day, every day. For 24 hours a day they had nothing to do but read a Bible to pass the time. The belief behind this system was that reflective time would change the inmates into repentant Christian men.

American prisons moved from a punitive model in the 1930s and 1940s, where little was done for the inmates and they were just kept out of sight and out of mind, to what was called the **medical model** beginning in the 1940s. This change was marked by a growing interest in psychology. The medical model saw offenders as ill or damaged and in need of treatment. Mental health programs, drug treatments, and educational programs began popping up in prisons in an effort to reform the inmates. The medical model is still very much alive today and we see it in many of the rehabilitative programs of corrections.

Beginning in the 1980s, overcrowding became a problem. Feeling the effects of tougher drug crimes and harsher sentences, America's prisons are busting at the seams. This overcrowding problem has led to **warehousing** of prisoners. This has taken the focus off of rehabilitative goals and started a move back towards incapacitation. Unfortunately this is largely due to the cost of running prisons to fill the needs of all of the offenders. Treatment programs, educators, and mental health professionals are all expensive. Correctional organizations struggle with doing what they would like to do (provide rehabilitative resources) with what they are forced to do (cut programs to afford more beds).

COMMUNITY CORRECTIONS

Also a member of the correctional family is community corrections. Community corrections include probation, parole, and other resources that allow offenders to remain in the community while serving out their sentence.

The largest sector of community corrections is **probation**. When a court sentences someone to probation it is often done because the judge believes the person will not be a risk to society if left within the community. A judge, along with state statute, spells out what will be the offender's conditions of probation, or rules he will have to follow. Probationers are supervised by an officer who they see on a regular basis. This officer ensures the offender is abiding by the terms set out by the court. The probationer may be required to attend treatment, perform community service, obtain a GED, or be on house arrest. The probation terms are determined not only by the crime that was committed but also by the characteristics of the offender. If a probationer violates the terms of probation, his officer can bring him back to court to have more sanctions imposed or possibly have his sentence "activated." This means that probation is a privilege and not a right. Typically a judge tells a probationer at sentencing that if they cannot abide by the terms of probation they will be brought back to court and face the original prison term that statute dictates for their crime.

Along with probation is another form of community supervision called **parole**. Parole is an early, supervised release from prison. Similar to probation, parolees are supervised by a parole officer and required to follow terms or rules of parole. If a parolee is found in violation of the terms of her parole, she can be returned to prison to finish the remainder of her sentence.

Along with the two above examples, there are many other forms of community corrections. Community corrections exist not only for the benefit of the offender, but also to relieve the overcrowding issues in American prisons.

CRIMINAL JUSTICE PROCESS

It is helpful to picture the criminal process as a funnel. Many people are cited and/or arrested but very few end up in prison. Entry into the system begins at the wide part of the funnel and ends at the bottom with the few who make it out through sentencing. Along the way the majority of cases are dropped, pled out, or resolved through some other means.

> **Warrants:** Warrants are documents signed by a judge authorizing the arrest of someone accused of a crime. Typically the police or state prosecutor supplies the judge with a sworn affidavit describing the alleged offense and outlining the probable cause. There must be probable cause present for a judge to sign an arrest warrant. Once the warrant is signed, it can be served and the accused can be taken into custody.

The criminal justice process typically begins with an arrest. This arrest may be because of a warrant or one that is made because the arrestee presents a current danger to himself or others. When a police officer places someone under arrest, he must advise her of her constitutional rights, called the **Miranda Rights**. At this point, typically, the offender will be transported to jail.

Shortly after arriving, however, offenders will have their first appearance in front of a judge. In most states the arraignment will happen within 24 hours of the arrest. This first appearance is referred to as the **arraignment**. At the arraignment the defendants will be advised of the charges against them and, depending on the severity of the crime, be asked if they wish to enter a plea. Most importantly, however, the judge will inform each defendant of some of his rights. Namely, the defendant will be informed of the right to counsel and the right against self incrimination.

What happens at the arraignment varies from state to state. The majority of states do not allow defendants charged with a felony to enter a plea at this point. Also, dependant on the charges, the judge may set bail. **Bail** is a way of ensuring the defendant will return to court for future proceedings. A defendant puts money up as a guarantee that they will return. For less serious crimes where the judge does not think the defendant is a "flight risk," he may release her on her own "recognizance." This is just a promise to return and is similar to bail in that regard, but no money or collateral is put up.

When charged with a felony, there will typically be a preliminary hearing. The preliminary hearing is an opportunity for both the prosecution and defense to present evidence. The goal of the preliminary hearing is *not* to determine guilt or innocence, but to determine if the prosecution has enough evidence to move to a trial. If there is sufficient evidence that a crime has been committed and the defendant was the person who did it (probable cause), the trial will go forward. If there isn't, the charges could be dropped.

> **Probable Cause:** Probable cause is a legal term used both in the courts and in the field by law enforcement officers. Many arrests and stages of prosecution cannot move forward if probable cause isn't present. Probable cause is simply a *reasonable* belief that someone committed a crime. It is a fairly low burden of proof when compared with "beyond a reasonable doubt" (used to determine guilt in criminal matters) or "preponderance of the evidence" (used in civil trials).

Between the preliminary hearing and trial date there can be many delays. **Continuances** will be filed to give either party more time for preparation. Motions will be filed for such things as admissibility of evidence or testimonies.

PLEA BARGAINING

Plea bargains can essentially happen at any stage of the court process. A **plea bargain** is when the defendant agrees to plead guilty to a lesser charge. Plea bargains may be used when the prosecution is not sure it can get a jury conviction on the original charges or when they don't think the charge warrants a trial. The defendant may choose to agree to a plea if she knows her case has problems. If someone is facing a 20-year sentence if convicted and thinks there is a good possibility she *will* be convicted, she will be more likely to readily accept a plea that offers her 5-10 years instead. Once a plea agreement is reached the prosecution will give a sentencing recommendation to the judge. Although judges are in no way bound to adhere to the prosecution's recommendations, they typically do in order to keep the potential defendant's faith in the sentence that a prosecutor offers in plea agreements.

Plea bargains are controversial. The reason they raise eyebrows is because they give the prosecutor power that has typically been handled by the judiciary and trial process. Essentially the prosecution decides who goes to trial and what sentence they will face through plea bargains and the choice of charges. Putting this much power into an individual who is biased (remember, this is an adversarial system) has caused many to question the integrity of the plea bargaining process. With nearly 95% of criminal cases ending in a plea agreement, it is no wonder the intentions of the prosecution are questioned.

JURY

The Sixth Amendment to the United States Constitution guarantees the right to trial by jury. Not all criminal cases result in jury trials, however. This is because the defendant, in most cases, can waive this right if she wishes and instead opt for a **bench trial** or one that is decided by the judge. In some states some misdemeanors are not eligible for jury trials. Early on in the trial process, jury selection begins. Referred to as **voir dire**, the jury selection process can be somewhat tedious. A jury pool is gathered and each side of the proceeding (defense and prosecution) has an opportunity to question and dismiss potential jurors.

The adversarial attorneys use challenges to remove people they do not want serving on the jury. There are three types of challenges used in jury selection.

1. Challenges to the array: when one side believes that the pool is not representative of the community or that it is biased.
2. Challenges for cause: making the argument that a specific juror may be biased and therefore impartial.
3. Peremptory Challenges: removal of a potential juror without having to show cause. This means that an attorney can remove a juror for no reason at all.

TRIAL

A criminal trial is adversarial and the defense and prosecution take turns in everything that is done. **Opening statements** are given by each side as an introduction to the case. The **presentation of evidence** is the longest part of the trial where each side calls witnesses and presents evidence. For each witness that is presented, each side has an opportunity to examine and cross-examine; going back and forth until both sides are satisfied. Once the presentation of evidence is complete, both sides will give closing arguments to the judge and/or jury. **Closing statements** sum up what has been presented and is when most attorneys try to convince the jury that they are right.

Before the jury retires to deliberate the judge will give them final instructions, often called the "judge's charge." All judges give charge a little differently. Most commonly, however, the judge will remind the jury of the criminal charges and elements of the crime. She will inform the jury of their role and need to unanimously find that the defendant is guilty "beyond a reasonable doubt." Some judges will comment on evidence and testimony at this time as well, essentially reviewing the cases that were presented before them.

Jury deliberations can last a few hours or several weeks. The jury is typically sequestered from outside influences and tasked with deciding the fate of the defendant. If a jury cannot reach a unanimous decision it is referred to as a "hung jury." If the jury is hung a mistrial may be declared. Prior to that, however, in an effort to move things forward, a judge may "re-charge" the jury, explaining the instructions and specifics of their duties once again. Sometimes this boost by the judge is all that is needed to move the deliberations along.

SENTENCING

Once the verdict has been reached and read, it is time for sentencing. Typically, especially in the case of felonies, a judge will set a future date for sentencing. One of the main reasons a judge will not sentence someone on the day of conviction is that a **pre-sentence investigation** must be completed.

Pre-sentence investigations are most commonly completed by probation officers in the community to determine if the defendant would be a good candidate for community supervision. The investigation and subsequent report is an in depth look at the defendant's life, both current and past. It will include such things as:

- Family history
- Psychological evaluation or history
- Connections in the community
- Employment history
- Criminal history
- Victim statements
- Circumstances of the offense

The investigating officer may interview family members, friends, and most likely the defendant himself. Once the investigation is complete and a report written, it will be given to the judge for review. The probation officer will typically make a recommendation in the report as to the chance of success the defendant might have if placed on probation. While the judge is under no obligation to follow the probation officer's recommendation, she will consider the professional experience and knowledge of the officer as relevant and helpful in making her decision.

When a judge sentences a convicted criminal, her options are not endless. Most states regulate sentences to a certain extent. The judge may be required to follow sentencing guidelines or recommendations as dictated by statute. While many of these sentencing guidelines were at one time mandatory, states and the federal government have moved to make them recommended sentences rather than hard and fast rules. This allows the judge to use her discretion when sentencing offenders, knowing that each crime and criminal is different and may require different sentencing to best protect society and give the criminal a better chance at reform. Following sentencing the convicted criminals serve out their sentences either in the community or in a correctional institution.

MEASURING CRIME

In order to successfully combat crime it must be measured and studied. There are several methods used to measure crime including self reporting surveys and data transmitted from law enforcement agencies around the country. While some of these sources of data are more reliable than others, they all have redeeming qualities.

NCVS

A self reporting survey is one that relies on crime victims to report incidences of crime. These have obvious drawbacks. Some victims do not report crimes either out of fear or because they may not consider what has happened to be a crime. One of the greatest difficulties with crime statistics is that quite often individuals who are the victim (or witness) of a crime will choose not to report it. This can occur for any number of reasons. One reason is when a person considers the crime too trivial to report. If a person sees someone illegally parked in front of a fire hydrant, they will most likely not report it because it is so insignificant. Another reason for not reporting a crime is when people feel that it won't do any good. If a person's jacket is stolen, for example, they may feel a coupling of the two – they may consider the jacket to be too insignificant to trouble the police about, and believe the chances of getting it back too small to be worth the effort. Occasionally there are situations where individuals are afraid to report a crime for fear of getting arrested themselves. This could be the case with prior criminals or illegal immigrants.

More serious reasons for not reporting crime include emotional trauma. With cases of rape or abuse this is often the case. It is estimated that 60% of rapes go unreported. Some reasons for this are that victims are too embarrassed or ashamed to admit the crime has occurred. Many are emotionally traumatized and react by ignoring the fact that it occurred. In situations of rape, abuse or domestic violence it is likely that the victim knows the person, and is afraid to speak out.

The National Crime Victimization Survey (NCVS) is one conducted by the Bureau of Justice Statistics. It was created in 1972 under President Lyndon B. Johnson's Commission on Law Enforcement and the Administration of Justice in an effort to uncover the dark figure of crime. The **dark figure of crime** refers to those crimes that go unreported to law enforcement and therefore are not measured.

The NCVS asks respondents a series of questions attempting to uncover if they have been victimized and how they have been victimized. The survey has been altered over the years to try to narrow down those crimes that go unreported, particularly domestic violence and incidents that plague fear-ridden neighborhoods.

The survey is sent out twice a year to citizens gathered from the U.S. Census. It covers all members of the household who are over twelve years of age. The survey is conducted six times over a period of three years. Twice the respondents are surveyed in person and four times the interview takes place over the phone. After three years, the pool of respondents changes.

UCR

Unlike the NCVS, the Uniform Crime Report relies on data supplied by law enforcement agencies throughout the country. The UCR is the primary body of data used when quoting crime rates and trends.

In the UCR, crimes are separated into one of two groups, Part I and Part II offenses. Part I offenses, also called **index crimes**, are the more serious of the two divisions and include offenses like: murder, rape, robbery, aggravated assault, larceny-theft, burglary, auto theft, and arson. These index crimes are further broken down into groups of *property* and *violent* crimes.

The UCR is compiled by the FBI annually. It is submitted to the FBI in two different ways, by crime reported and by crime resolved with an arrest. Crime that is resolved with an arrest is known as the **clearance rate**.

Participation in the UCR is not mandatory and although the majority of large law enforcement agencies comply with it, there are still some who do not. Also, of those who comply, uniformity in data collection can be a problem. By reporting more crimes police departments may qualify for more government funding to combat crime. This loophole invites dishonesty into the UCR and makes some question as to how reliable the compiled data really is.

NIBRS

The most recent addition to crime data collection is the **National Incident-Based Reporting System** (NIBRS) conducted by the Bureau of Justice Statistics and established in 1988. This system is similar to the UCR in that the data is reported by law enforcement.

The NIBRS categorizes crimes into two groups similar to the UCR, group A and group B, with group B including the more serious crimes of the two. The NIBRS includes drug crimes, which is a serious improvement over the UCR, which doesn't include drug offenses at all.

Although the NIBRS does have some edge over the UCR, due to its relatively recent creation, many towns, cities, and states are still in the process of testing and adopting it for use. It is a voluntary program as well.

VICTIMLESS CRIME

A victimless crime is any crime which does not harm another person or their property, and which does not infringe on the rights of another individual. Victimless crimes are sometimes referred to as consensual crimes. Some examples of victimless crimes include prostitution, gambling, consumption of illegal drugs, and euthanasia. In each case the act is illegal, although the person committing the crime is not directly infringing on the rights of others. While some victimless crimes tend to go unnoticed, others are more heavily enforced. For example, many people gamble, such as by betting with friends on the outcome of football games, without repercussion. On the other hand, prostitution and drunk driving are heavily enforced.

Victimless crimes constitute a large portion of arrests each year, with around four hundred arrests each year relating to victimless or consensual crimes. It is estimated that approximately 350,000 individuals are currently in jail for the commission of victimless crimes. The most common victimless crimes are those relating to drug use. The Bureau of Justice Statistics reports that just over half of all individuals in prison are there as a result of drug related crimes.

 Police Systems in the United States

Police systems in the United States are broken down by jurisdiction or by the laws they enforce and the areas in which they enforce them.

FEDERAL LAW ENFORCEMENT

HOMELAND SECURITY

The Secret Service has two areas of responsibility. These are protecting the President and other important governmental leaders (including the Vice President, former Presidents and visiting dignitaries), and investigating various treasury related matters such as counterfeiting, money laundering and securities fraud. The Secret Service operates under the Department of Homeland Security.

U.S. MARSHALS

Federal Law Enforcement Agencies began with the development of the U.S. Marshals. The position of marshal was created in 1789 by the first President, George Washington. As the United States grew, the marshals became the main arm of law enforcement in the early territories. For the early American citizens, the marshals represented the federal government in their communities.

Now, however, U.S. Marshals, still under the office of the attorney general, are less visible but still a useful presence. There are 94 marshals, one for each federal judicial district. These marshals appoint a number of Deputy Marshals to carry out duties under them. The marshals and deputies have several responsibilities including apprehending federal fugitives, protecting the federal judges, operating the witness protection program, and handling seized property from federal criminals. Marshals also handle the transfer of dangerous offenders from state to state and country to country for extradition.

FBI

The Federal Bureau of Investigation is the most well known federal law enforcement agency. Created in 1908 and originally referred to as the Bureau of Investigation, the FBI served as the investigative branch of the Department of Justice. It was originally created to help thwart the rising crime in politics and business.

Although it was created nearly twenty years earlier, the FBI really began gaining notoriety when J. Edgar Hoover was appointed director in 1924. Hoover moved the FBI toward the professional organization it is today. The FBI only recruited college graduates, and the new agents were thoroughly trained and assigned on a national basis. It was under Hoover that the FBI became the clearinghouse for criminal information and data, compiling records and the fingerprint database.

The FBI has grown both in numbers and powers over its term of existence. Today the FBI focuses on a multitude of crimes. The FBI is also in charge of collecting and handling the data collected in the Uniform Crime Report (UCR). It maintains the national fingerprint database and millions of criminal records in the NCIC. The FBI also serves to assist other law enforcement agencies, federal and otherwise, in certain investigations and by volunteering the use of its state-of-the-art laboratory. Providing training to thousands on the application of their services like the UCR collection, NCIC usage and fingerprinting, the FBI can be more assured of uniformity in the use of these systems.

According to the FBI, their purpose includes the following:

1. To protect the U.S. from terrorist attacks
2. To protect the U. S. against foreign espionage
3. To protect the U. S. against cyber-based attacks and high-tech offenses
4. To combat public corruption
5. To protect the civil rights of U.S. citizens
6. To combat criminal organizations and enterprises
7. To combat major white-collar crime
8. To combat significant violent crime
9. To support federal, state, local and international partners
10. To upgrade technology in order to successfully perform the FBI's mission

DRUG ENFORCEMENT AGENCY (DEA)

The DEA had its start in 1914 with the Harrison Narcotic Act under President Woodrow Wilson, which prohibited the possession of illegal drugs such as heroin and morphine by an "unregistered person." Acting under the early IRS, this agency was originally referred to as a Miscellaneous Division. With the Volstead Act passed in 1919, the Prohibition unit was created in the IRS. Within the Prohibition unit was a Narcotics Division. The Narcotics Division grew to serve the United States from thirteen national offices. Again changing its name in 1930, the now Federal Bureau of Narcotics was under the direction of Harry J. Anslinger and grew very quickly. After many name changes and reorganizations, the Drug Enforcement Agency was officially created in 1973 with the Reorganization Plan Number 2, which consolidated several drug enforcement forces under one agency.

Today the DEA is one of the largest Federal law enforcement agencies. They serve to:

1. Investigate and prepare for the prosecution of major drug offenders operating at interstate and international levels.
2. Investigate and prepare for prosecution of criminals and drug gangs.
3. Manage a national drug intelligence program in cooperation with federal, state, local, and foreign officials.
4. Enact seizure and forfeiture of assets derived from illicit drug trafficking.
5. Enforce the provisions of the Controlled Substances Act.
6. Coordinate with federal, state and local law enforcement officials on mutual drug enforcement efforts.

7. Coordinate and cooperate with other law enforcement agencies and foreign countries in an effort to reduce the availability of illicit abuse-type drugs on the United States market.
8. Liaison with the United Nations and other organizations on matters relating to international drug control programs.

IMMIGRATION AND CUSTOMS ENFORCEMENT (ICE)

Created recently in 2003 by combining the former Treasury departments of Immigration and Naturalization Services and Customs Enforcement, the Immigration and Customs Enforcement is now an investigative branch of the Department of Homeland Security. ICE attempts to effectively enforce immigration and customs law in an effort to protect the United States. Through the targeting of illegal immigrants, the protecting of U.S. borders, and the enforcement of custom law, ICE's main goal is the prevention of terrorist attacks. This is a change in focus since the attacks on the United States on September 11, 2001. ICE still serves many enforcement goals that were shared by the organizations that made it up. Some of the other duties of ICE are:

1. Dismantling gang organizations.
2. Investigating employers and targeting illegal workers who have gained access to important worksites like nuclear plants, airports, etc.
3. Identifying fraudulent immigration applications and fraudulent illegal document manufacture.
4. Investigating the illegal export of U.S. munitions and sensitive technology.
5. Combating criminal organizations that smuggle and traffic in humans across our borders.
6. Ensuring that every illegal immigrant who has been ordered removed departs the U.S. as quickly as possible.
7. Seeking to eliminate the financial system that criminal organizations use to earn, move and keep money.
8. Providing law enforcement and security services to federal buildings.
9. Targeting criminal organizations responsible for producing, smuggling and distributing counterfeit products.

STATE LAW ENFORCEMENT AGENCIES

Beginning long ago with the Texas Rangers, state law enforcement agencies are an important part of the law enforcement community. Because the states are allowed to develop state law enforcement agencies as they see fit, there are many different organizational quirks from state to state dependant on their unique needs and requirements.

There are two organizational models that *most* state law enforcement agencies fall into. These are the decentralized and centralized models.

A **centralized model** (also referred to as having *general* police powers) means simply that all of the state law enforcement duties fall under one heading, whether that heading be the Michigan State Police of the Pennsylvania State Police. These agencies have their traffic enforcement, investigative, and all other enforcement capabilities under their singular umbrella.

These agencies have goals such as:

- Assisting local law enforcement with criminal investigations when necessary
- Maintaining criminal records
- Patrolling the state highways

The centralization of all of the state law enforcement duties allows these states a more streamlined structure with fewer "cooks in the kitchen."

A **decentralized model**, however, may have several organizations all acting essentially separately from one another in their goals and duties. For example, the California Highway Patrol handles all traffic enforcements and accidents while the California State Police is responsible for protecting state property. Another example is North Carolina, which has the North Carolina Highway Patrol for state traffic enforcement, and the State Bureau of Investigation, which handles all criminal investigative matters under the state's jurisdiction.

Decentralized state law enforcement may also have several adjunct agencies for other law enforcement duties. The state of North Carolina, for example, has a State Wildlife Commission, board of Alcohol Beverage Control, and an Enforcement and Theft Bureau in addition to their state patrol and state investigative agency. By separating the powers through several agencies the decentralized states hope to provide those agencies with a more specialized structure.

LOCAL LAW ENFORCEMENT AGENCIES

Like state agencies, local agencies vary widely across the country. "Local" law enforcement is a broad topic that would include city police departments, county sheriff's departments, as well as campus police and parking enforcements, to name a few.

SHERIFF'S DEPARTMENTS

At one time the majority of local agencies were sheriff's departments and these departments were responsible for all enforcement on the local level. However, now sheriff's departments are far more limited in their duties and responsibilities. Sheriffs are typically elected officials who oversee deputies and other support staff. These departments may be responsible for serving summonses and other court documents as well as providing security in courthouses and courtrooms. Sheriff's Departments are also responsible for running county jails in communities across the country. The majority of sheriff's offices across the United States are very small and have very limited powers. Some agencies serve solely as courthouse security while other larger offices may run county jails with populations well into the thousands. Still in some smaller counties in the West and South, the sheriff's department is still the main local law enforcement agency serving not only traffic enforcement purposes but also criminal investigations.

CITY POLICE DEPARTMENTS

City departments are led by Police Chiefs who are typically appointed by the mayor or sometimes chosen by a city council. Depending on the size of the city, the city police department may number well into the thousands. Like all other local agencies, however, organizational models differ greatly.

The most well recognized municipal law enforcement agency in the United States is the New York Police Department whose sworn officers number well over 30,000, making it the largest in the world. More prone to controversy, solely due to its size, the New York Police Department is still recognized as being one of the best both in function and training.

SPECIALIZED LOCAL LAW ENFORCEMENT

Depending on the size of the city in question, many smaller agencies can exist to serve in some law enforcement capacity. The City of New York is a good example of this. New York has several specialized law enforcement branches. The Transit Authority is responsible for enforcement on the city's mass public transportation systems. New York also has an additional arm of the police in the Housing Authority Police, tasked with law enforcement within the large system of public housing.

Another example of specialized law enforcement is that of campus police on college campuses across the country. By delegating responsibilities to smaller specialized agencies, large cities can provide law enforcement specifically geared to the problem areas it may have. These smaller forces typically have the authority to arrest as well as other rights granted to the regular police force.

PRIVATE INDUSTRY IN POLICING

Not a new development, but certainly a growing one is the role of private security and law enforcement companies. Private law enforcement has grown considerably both in numbers and in quality over the past few decades. Private businesses and companies look to private security to protect their interests when they cannot depend on the local police. Local police cannot be responsible for what is happening at all times in every place under their jurisdiction, the numbers and costs simply don't allow it. By hiring private security, companies can rest assured that their property will be guarded when the police can't be there.

ROLE OF POLICE

The police have served the role of law enforcers for centuries. However, their roles within their respective communities require more of them than simple arrests. The police have many different responsibilities dependant on the needs of their communities and the expectations of the citizens.

The roles of police are:

1. Enforce laws
2. Keep the peace
3. Prevent crimes
4. Protect rights
5. Provide services

While more specific roles are common and varied throughout the country, these are the universally accepted roles of police in general.

ENFORCE LAWS

The most widely accepted role of the police is as law enforcement. We expect the police to investigate and apprehend criminals when they break the law. While this role is a long-standing one, it has changed and become more complex with the passage of time. No longer are police simply arresting people who commit crimes, but now they are acting as an integral part of the criminal justice system, balancing many issues and interpretations when acting in this role.

Enforcing laws includes many items in the job duties of an officer. Included under this role are:

- Investigating offenses
- Questioning suspects
- Conducting searches
- Patrolling
- Interviewing witnesses
- Testifying in court
- Acting on leads
- Performing stake-outs

In the days of early America, a citizen could be arrested if the officer thought he had committed a crime. While the same is true today, modern day police are required to know the laws they enforce and make decisions based on statutory powers. A police officer who uses force outside an acceptable range could lose his job or freedom. Likewise his supervisors and the citizens he serves will not be pleased if he uses his power in a manner not consistent with the expectations of the people. What this means is that now the police are required to hold themselves to a very high level of professionalism. By becoming an "integral part of the criminal justice process," the police now must act with greater vigilance and intelligence than ever before.

By acting as the entrance to the criminal justice system, officers must be sure to act in a manner consistent with the wishes of the municipality (or state or country) as stated in statute and precedence. Acting within these laws and wishes, the police gain the respect of the public as professionals capable of initiating the criminal justice process where appropriate.

Police cannot enforce all laws at all times. Because there are a limited number of police officers, there is no way that all crimes will end in an arrest or conviction. The majority of people understand and accept this but do rely on the police to be a visible fixture within the community acting as the "crime fighters" we make them out to be. This role of the police satisfies the public's need to feel safe, if handled correctly.

KEEPING THE PEACE

The role of peacekeeper allows the police to intervene in non-criminal situations. Unique about this role is that the success of the police in fulfillment of this role depends wholly on the public acceptance of them. Because this role is activated typically in non-criminal situations, citizens *allow* the police to intervene in these circumstances where statute doesn't *require* them to.

For instance, if two neighbors frequently argue about their property line, a police officer acting as a peacekeeper may meet with the neighbors and suggest solutions to their conflict. She may visit with both people and try to get them to work something out for the good of the community. If either neighbor doesn't want to listen to the officer, they don't have to and can carry on their petty arguments. However, if both citizens give the officer's role respect and listen, considering what the officer has to say, her role at peacekeeper could be fulfilled.

If the community does not respect the police, their peacekeeping role can be seriously damaged. Looking at some high violence inner-city neighborhoods, you can see this. The people have become so distrustful of the police that any attempts at keeping the peace, or serving a role other than "law enforcement" is usually an uphill battle.

Keeping the peace is directly related to the goal of enforcing the laws. The reason for this is because often these non-criminal situations, if not dealt with on the peacekeeping level, will become criminal matters.

PREVENTING CRIMES

Closely related to the roles discussed thus far is crime prevention. The role of preventing crimes can be fulfilled *through* keeping the peace. However, crime prevention is different from peacekeeping and law enforcement in that it seeks to stop potentially dangerous and criminal acts from happening.

On a small scale, stopping a robbery in progress is preventing crime. However, on a larger scale, that arrest could deter future robberies from taking place, preventing crimes of an unknown number. One of the difficulties with this role of the police is that it is often immeasurable. Sure, the police can count how many crimes in progress they stopped. What can't be counted, however, are those potential crimes that were either directly or indirectly prevented.

Police know that preventing crime works, regardless of the lack of measurement. They attempt to fulfill this goal through many avenues. Cooperating with and educating the community to create neighborhood watch groups prevents an untold number of crimes. Being visible is another way that police prevent crimes. Police frequently increase visibility in problem areas because they know their presence will prevent crimes from occurring.

Proactive policing is a systematic attempt at preventing crime before it happens. *Reactive* policing is when the police respond to calls, making arrest and dealing with crimes after they happen. Over the past several decades, proactive policing has taken hold. It is an effort by the officers to get out in the community and act before the calls come in. By being *a part of* the community they serve, the police can deter future crimes rather than only reacting to crimes already committed.

PROTECTING RIGHTS

The police have an obligation to protect the constitutional rights of the people they serve. This proves to be ironic, as one of the greatest powers of law enforcement is that of arrest, the constitutionally allowed *removal* of rights. Because of this role it is important that police officers understand the constitutional rights they are charged with protecting. Police take safeguards everyday that they are protecting our rights. From reading an arrestee their "Miranda rights" to stopping questioning if a suspect requests an attorney, the police know their roles as law enforcement and protector of rights must exist simultaneously.

When the police fail to protect someone's Constitutional rights we hear about it. Oftentimes a case will make it to court and charges may be dropped because of an oversight on the part of the police, allowing an accused criminal to get off "on a technicality."

PROVIDING SERVICES

The commonly-used phrase, "To serve and protect," service to the community is an important role of the police. Services that the police provide range from giving directions, to assisting with licensing and inspecting vehicles. Police intervene in domestic arguments and render emergency assistance on a daily basis. These acts may not be explicitly laid out in the police manual but are considered services provided by many forces.

Debate exists on how great a service role the police should take. On one hand is the argument that the police must serve the public in roles other than law enforcement to prevent crimes and gain public respect. On the other hand is the school of thought that states the police should not serve as a community service organization and that they should stick to the role of law enforcement and crime prevention.

Because the police are often the most available government representatives in the community, they are called on to do many things that would be better carried out by other agencies. This is to be expected due to their visibility and accessibility.

Some common community services provided by law enforcement are:

- Emergency first aid
- Dispute resolution and mediation
- Escort services (for celebrities and politicians)
- Assistance getting into locked vehicles and homes
- Missing persons
- Missing animals
- Damage to property

The police understand, for the most part, that by fulfilling these roles that go beyond the normal call of duty they increase their visibility and respect within the communities. By participating in the community they gain the respect that might otherwise be missing.

If police took a more aloof attitude to community service, their effectiveness at crime reduction and law enforcement could be seriously damaged. This is particularly evident in high crime neighborhoods that are missing the respect for law enforcement. Because the police are only seen as the force behind arrests, the community does not honor them in any service role. They become a power that is seen as taking *from* the community rather than contributing to it or participating in it.

Police Organization

Organizational styles of police departments vary slightly across the country but for the most part they follow the same basic structure. Police department employees can typically be separated into two distinct categories: line or field services and administrative staff.

LINE STAFF/FIELD SERVICES

Line staff (also referred to as field services) refers to the police department employees who work in the field or the ones who are "on the line" in a typical work day. These are the people we automatically think of when we hear the term "police." This group includes uniformed officers and investigative staff (detectives). They directly enforce the law.

Line staff is responsible for:

- Patrol
- Community services
- Traffic enforcement
- Investigations

Typically the structure of line staff is militaristic with officers being the lowest rank, reporting to Sergeants. Lieutenants and Majors would report directly to the Chief. Of course, depending on the size of the department, not all ranks may be present in the line staff.

Patrol officers typically account for the majority of line staff. This is where most departments spend the most money as well. These are the primary points of contact with the community and those that we think of when we picture our local police.
Patrol are typically uniformed and in marked cars (or motorcycles). They are responsible for responding to dispatch calls and providing crime deterrence, emergency assistance, and criminal apprehension.

Traffic enforcement may be included with patrol but in some bigger cities, traffic is a separate group of staff. They are responsible for directing and controlling traffic, responding to accidents, citing traffic offenses, and providing assistance to motorists.

Investigation staff is another term for detectives. These individuals typically were raised through the patrol ranks to join an elite group of detectives specializing in a specific area of investigation. They are not usually uniformed and travel in unmarked cars.

Responsibilities of investigative staff include: securing crime scenes, interviewing witnesses, gathering and recording all evidence, processing crime scenes, and questioning suspects. Larger forces have specialized units for crime scene processing, but it is the investigative staff that are responsible for the security of the scene. Investigators work directly with patrol in their duties. This collaboration is required for a successful operation.

Community service staff within the force may have their own division or it may be a role left for patrol to pick up. While patrol officers no doubt have a community service role, some larger departments have created a niche staff that is completely dedicated to serving the community. These people may lead crime prevention programs, outreach events, and act as a direct channel to the top for the citizens.

Administrative staff includes everyone else employed by the department. These are all of the people that may be behind the scenes but nonetheless are vital in the running of a successful police department.

Administrative staff may include the following:

- Training
- Laboratory staff
- Research and planning
- Communications
- Records
- Internal affairs

Training staff has come a long way in the past several decades. With the professionalization of police, came a need for top-of-the-line training. Many training staff were once line staff. The academies responsible for training new recruits can draw from this experience and provide quality curriculum for the recruits. Larger forces will employ staff certified in teaching in order for trainees to get the most out of a training program.

This training staff knows that the content they teach is very serious in the lives of many citizens that will come to depend on the new officers at one time or another. For this reason, the lessons must be relevant and useful.

Laboratory staff are those that perform tests on evidence from crime scenes. The investigative line staff depends on the lab for meticulous attention to detail and work that is virtually mistake free.

Records personnel are responsible for managing the paperwork of the entire department. This doesn't just refer to criminal records, but administrative records, identification records and complaints as well. An efficient records staff is a vital tool in an efficient and reliable force.

With technology booming, some forces are slowly making a move to "paperless" records. This reduces the amount of waste and ensures that pieces of information are less likely to get lost or mishandled.

Communications staff has many responsibilities in police departments. They answer dispatch calls and conduct radio transmissions to field staff. Along with this is the responsibility of keeping line staff informed of what is going on in their community and within the department.

Radio is still the primary method of communication in police forces. A typical radio program has four channels for use. One channel is for patrol staff to communicate with each other, one is for patrol to contact dispatch, one allows the patrol to contact officers that may be in another jurisdiction, and finally is a channel for emergency calls. These separate channels are needed to ensure that there is an avenue open for communication at all times.

Research and planning departments are in charge of looking at data and allocating funds. They may come up with staffing solutions and how to make budget cuts work. In an industry where funds are limited, the research and planning team must be on the ball.

PROFESSIONALIZATION OF LAW ENFORCEMENT

Only within the last century has law enforcement begun to take on the role of a true profession. This is not to say that law enforcement officers prior to the last century weren't professional. However, more recently through accreditations and certifications, degree programs, and by gaining an overall greater respect by the public, the police have moved into a better light.

What separates jobs and professions is a skilled workforce. If your workforce has to possess a certain skill or ability they may be acting in a professional manner. When a "job" has certain requirements for new hires it increases its professional air. For example, teaching requires a degree and certain skills. The fact that not everyone can get a job teaching makes it a profession. Add to that accreditation or professional certification, and not only will they have the professional title, but also the public respect that goes with it.

Thinking back to the era of thief takers, we realize that volunteer law enforcement, which could be done by *anyone*, could not be considered a profession. Likewise night watchmen in early America could not be referred to as professionals in their field. In the 1800-1900s police agencies took a turn for the better. Simple solutions like uniforms helped increase the force's professionalism in the eyes of the people. Along with appearance, however, professional behavior was needed to further professionalize the field.

In the early 1900's August Vollmer led the way to professionalization of America's police by requiring psychological and intelligence testing in the recruitment process. Although it wasn't a requirement at the time, he also began recruiting college graduates onto the force in Berkeley. This era was marked by a slow move toward increasing standards in the recruiting and hiring stages.

TRAINING

Later, in the 1950s, professionalization was furthered through training. By educating the officers, not only did the police departments gain respect, but they also increased their chances at being effective in law enforcement. Many forces began requiring a certain number of college credit hours for their new trainees. Often these credits were earned in a police academy setting. By employing professionals to train the new recruits, departments could be assured that their newest police officers would have the knowledge necessary to make good choices and decisions while working.

ACCREDITATION

In a collaborative effort at widespread professionalization, top law enforcement practitioners met in 1979 and formed the Commission on Accreditation for Law Enforcement Agencies (CALEA). Unlike attempts before, this board was made up of respected police professionals from around the country. In addition to the law enforcement expertise that makes up CALEA are several respected people in the criminal justice community including judges, elected officials, and members of academia. CALEA is still in existence today, offering voluntary accreditation to law enforcement agencies in the United States.

In order to be accredited through the CALEA, a law enforcement agency must meet several standards as dictated by the CALEA accreditation process. These standards are numerous and address issues such as:

- Personnel processing and structure
- Organization and management
- Relationships with other agencies
- Roles and responsibilities
- Operations
- Traffic operations
- Prisoner and court-related activities
- Auxiliary services

Accreditation through CALEA is completely voluntary, but has become a well known and respected method of professionalization within the law enforcement community.

ENTRANCE TESTING

One of the standards of CALEA accreditation used throughout the country is the requirement that all applicants are required to take intelligence, psychological, and physical tests prior to their hiring. What started in Berkeley with Vollmer has become a national standard. Recruits will be tested in most forces to ensure that they are intelligent enough to handle the knowledge required of police officers. They will be tested to ensure that they can comply with the physical demands of the job and will also be evaluated to ensure that they can deal with the emotional stress of this highly stressful profession.

EDUCATIONAL STANDARDS

While few forces require new hires to have a college degree, many of them do require some college credits. They also encourage staff to return to school and further their education. Through a Department of Justice agency called Law Enforcement Assistance Administration, departments were able to get funding for the education of their staff. This agency was later abolished in 1982. However, police agencies continue to offer tuition assistance in encouragement of a higher education. Recruits with college degrees may have more clout when it comes time for hiring and later, promotions.

PROMOTIONAL STANDARDS

In the past, during years of rampant corruption, promotions were often given on the basis of who you were, who you knew, or who liked you. Now, however, promotions are often weighed against a comprehensive set of standards. Much care is taken to ensure that those officers or staff being promoted are fit to fill the shoes of a higher level position. Depending on the agency, promotions may include testing and oral interviews. In alignment with CALEA standards, many larger forces have set up "assessment centers" solely for the purpose of practicing better promotional procedures.

When promoting, agencies want to be certain of three things:

1. They are choosing the best person with the best skill set and knowledge for the position.
2. The promotional process is fair and objective.
3. The promotion would be defensible in court and reduces the likelihood of grievances and appeals.

The public's perception of the police department is directly related to the department's success in fulfilling its roles. A professional agency that strives to be seen in a good light is one that will gain the respect of the citizens it serves, thereby increasing the department's success and ease with which the officer's duties can be carried out.

POLICE SUBCULTURE

Police officers and those within the law enforcement field have a culture all their own. From the way they talk to their outlook on society, police are often a little outside the norm. It is important to look at how police interact with each other and how they interact with their families and members of their community outside the force.

Many studies have been done on how police interact with each other and the culture of law enforcement while on the job. What a new officer learns in a training academy can vary greatly with what they will learn once they are on the streets practicing their job. It is on the job that officers learn what it means to be "streetwise," or the balance between what is viewed acceptable by the administration through policies and procedures, and what is deemed acceptable by fellow officers. In most situations this range is not that great. Meaning, the looser version of "acceptable" does not stray *too* far from policy. Jobs in law enforcement are best learned by doing. Because of this departments usually employ a fairly lengthy term of on-the-job training. When a rookie begins his job he is usually paired with a veteran who will say something like, "Now you'll learn what the job is *really* about." It is through discussions with veterans and other new recruits that a rookie will develop his "working personality."

ISOLATION

Because law enforcement is such a unique field, police are often isolated from friendships outside the circle of the field. Officers may work strange hours and not be available on weekends. They also feel more comfortable relaxing with people who understand their job and experience stresses similar to theirs. This can lead officers to abandon friendships from the past in an effort to build stronger relationships within the force. More and more officers will find themselves spending their off hours with the same people they work with. Spouses will become friends and their children will play together. This separation of law enforcement officers from the general public may not be conscious or intentional but it is certainly a reality.

STRESS

It is a widely accepted fact that law enforcement is one of the most stressful occupations in the world. Long term stress can be debilitating and lead to health problems and burnout. The stress experienced in this field can have long term physical, emotional, and psychological effects.

There are four different kinds of stressors in police work:

1. Personal stress
2. External stress
3. Organizational stress
4. Operational stress

Personal stressors within law enforcement refer to those that may come from relationships with other officers. Friendships marked by extremely strong bonds have the potential to cause extreme stress. A conflict with another officer can cause immediate stress but can also draw further criticism and stress from other officers or administration. Friendships among police go far beyond typical acquaintances because officers must balance their friendship with their ability to perform highly structured work.

External stressors are those that are truly unique to the field. Responding to calls where there is the potential for violence or danger causes an immediate stress response by raising the heart rate and dumping adrenaline. But, what about those situations that truly impact officers forever? Officers will witness events that can forever change them. Dealing with the death of a child or witnessing an assault on another officer can haunt a person indefinitely. Certainly the anticipation of something tragic is constantly in the back of an officer's mind. This steady, constant stress can impact the officer just as greatly as a one-time traumatic occurrence.

Organizational stress refers to stress that is caused by the many demands of being a police officer. Completing paperwork, scheduling training, writing reports, and adhering to scheduling can all cause an officer to push his organizational and time management skills to a new level. It is not rare for officers to have to work late when overtime is not authorized simply because they are expected to do too much in any given day. What may be realistic expectations on one day, will be far too much on a day when call volume is tremendous.

Operational stress is the constant level of stress that is present when an officer must deal with combating crime on a daily basis. The police see humankind often at its worst. This day-to-day functioning that revolves around negativity can produce a steady stream of stress often undetected by the person experiencing it. This stress, because it is a normal occurrence, can be particularly dangerous as it may cause a person to slowly change his personality and outlook on life.

Although stress is not unique to law enforcement, the level of it and the acknowledgement of it are. Because of the macho attitude that is still held by much of law enforcement, acknowledging stress can be nearly impossible for officers.

Within the past several decades much has been done in the way of stress management for law enforcement professionals. When single traumatic events take place a department will often evaluate the officers involved and watch for signs of extreme stress. Most large departments include a mental health department to assist officers who may be having a difficult time. A move by administration toward acknowledging the stress of the job has helped officers avoid burnout and mental health problems to a great extent.

Although police work can be a highly rewarding career, it can also have a number of negative effects within the officer's family. The main problem which most officers' families typically face is stress–in various forms. One cause of stress in an officer's home life results from crazy work schedules. Officer's may have constantly changing shifts, and can be required to work long hours. This creates difficulty in coordinating with family members and can be a barrier to effective communication. Another cause of stress originates from the officer simply carrying out their duties. Police officers tend to be exposed to more traumatic, dangerous and difficult situations than the average person. As a result, many can become cynical, overprotective or detached. This can be a barrier to having meaningful relationships and conversations. On top of these many stress causing factors, there is also the added stress to an officer's family of knowing that he could possibly be killed in the line of duty

SECRECY IN POLICING

The high stress nature of police jobs creates a bond among officers that is unique. Often you will hear police refer to each other as "brothers" or "sisters." Unique opportunities for bonding create strong friendships and extreme loyalty. While this support within the force is usually positive, it can create a loyalty that turns a blind eye to negative behavior.

What is often referred to as the "blue code" or the "blue wall" is a figurative wall that separates the police from the rest of society. When referring to the blue code we are often talking about a code of secrecy. When an officer is accused of wrongdoing, many times, none of his fellow officers will come forward to assist with an investigation against him (or her). The loyalty between police is often so strong that they will allow one bad apple to get away with wrongdoing rather than break the "code." This code of silence and air of secrecy has lent itself quite readily to corruption.

POLICE DEVIANCE AND CORRUPTION

With considerable authority comes the risk for abuse. Power is a valuable commodity and one that humans have the tendency to abuse if not held in check. Abuse of power is one of the leading causes of police corruption. **Corruption** is defined as deviation from an accepted ethical standard. What constitutes corruption, however, is not always that simple to define.

Characterized as a "slippery slope," what is considered police corruption is difficult to determine. Where does simple favor end and corruption begin? This is a question not easily answered. For this reason, many departments do not allow officers to even take a free cup of coffee from the café on their patrol. The worry is that an occasional cup of coffee could turn into an everyday cup of coffee or more, which could leave an officer feeling in debt to a citizen or leave a citizen feeling entitled to special treatment by the police.

In an effort to define what constitutes deviance, there are two distinctions: **occupational deviance** and **abuse of authority**. Occupational deviance refers to acts that are motivated by personal benefit. Abuse of authority includes those actions that happen in furthering the goals of law enforcement. For example, accepting that cup of coffee from the café down the street might be occupational deviance. However, overlooking the fact that the café owner is allowing drugs to be sold out of the café in exchange for money would be an extreme abuse of power.

In a well known example of police corruption and a trial that brought down the blue code of silence for a time in New York, Frank Serpico of the New York City Police Department testified in front of the Knapp Commission to uncover a large complex corruption ring. Later made into a famous movie, Serpico's 1971 testimony made it glaringly clear there was a need for greater accountability and control to combat corruption.

THE LURE OF CORRUPTION

Although there are countless reasons an individual officer might become corrupt, a few common factors increase the likelihood.

1. Exposure to criminality
2. Lure of money
3. Street smarts

Police are exposed daily to a side of the population many of us never see. They are immersed in the criminal world, becoming familiar with the people and actions that are prevalent in that world. This daily exposure can alter the officer's view of the criminal world. The resulting tolerance to criminality can make it easier for an officer to justify his own criminal acts.

Law enforcement is not a high paying job. For the risks that abound in police work, officers should be compensated healthily. However, due to budget constraints and the fact that it is a government job and not a private industry, salaries are limited. Corruption offers police an additional income. Depending on how deep an officer is willing to go, this additional income can be quite lucrative.

Police know how the streets work. They know ways around being caught and this street smarts can lead an officer to believe that he is beyond the reach of law enforcement. Because he knows how the department works and how criminals get caught, a corrupt police officer can use his connections in the criminal world to get ahead.

COMBATING CORRUPTION

An obvious solution to corruption is instilling ethical practices and education into line staff through training. Achieving that goal, however, poses a greater problem. If a person is likely to become corrupt, will any amount of training help? There are several ways departments have found to be effective at fighting corruption within the ranks.

The U.S. Department of Justice came up with a series of methods to combat corruption in law enforcement. Those methods include: managerial solutions, changing the task environment, and changing the political environment.

The Department of Justice defined **managerial solutions** as those that administration could perform through a number of "hands on" strategies. Those strategies include:

1. Staff turnover
2. Accountability
3. Close supervision of supervisors
4. Ending corrupted practices

Staff turnover was not about firing old staff and bringing in new, but rather constantly moving staff around. By bringing new staff in and rotating existing staff to new departments or new geographical areas, the officers were kept fresh. Investigations had shown that when police were in a position or certain patrol area for a long period of time, they were more susceptible to participation in corrupt practices.

Accountability referred to the need to hold officers and all police staff responsible for their actions. Supervisors that refused to be accountable for their own actions and the actions of officers below them were seen as poor risk managerial material. Supervisors had to be personally invested in combating corruption within the force.

Officers weren't the only ones with corrupt practices. **Close supervision of supervisors** was needed to make sure they were practicing in ethical ways. In order for an officer to be corrupt either the supervisor was turning a blind eye or was not interested enough in her job to make the officer's work her business. Supervisors often allowed corrupt practices if they paid off in the long run. By watching supervisory practices closely, administration could discourage corruption and encourage accountability.

Ending corrupt practices sought to do away with legal policies that encouraged unethical behaviors. These practices included arrest quotas and reimbursement for personal on-the-job expenses. The Department of Justice saw these practices as causing officers to blur the line between ethics and corruption.

Changing the task environment refers to changing the environment surrounding the officers that encouraged corruption. These environmental factors may not have seemed corrupt in themselves but blurred the already unclear line between what was acceptable and what was not. For instance, in an effort to change the task environment, police departments could make a plea to public businesses to stop offering gifts to the officers. As discussed earlier, a free cup of coffee could easily turn into a favor down the line. By educating the public on the progression of corruption, agencies could hope to decrease these small incidents that could lead to more serious offenses.

Changing the political environment was what the Department of Justice called those incidents of political favor. When a member of the city council could have a speeding ticket dropped, or even a DWI charge because of "who" they were, it was corrupting the ethics of law enforcement. Essentially no one is above the law, and changing the political environment called for equal enforcement and an end to favoritism. Corrupt politicians can have a great influence on the police; for this reason, they cannot co-exist with an *ethical* police force.

INTERNAL AFFAIRS

The Department of Justice came up with these effective ways of combating corruption. But, certainly there are other methods as well. One of the biggest developments in combating corruption was the development of Internal Affairs departments within the police departments around the country. Although to the officers who believe in the "blue code of silence," these departments were akin to a deep betrayal, they have significantly decreased undetected corruption in police agencies.

With the development and improvement of Internal Affairs units came an encouragement to be open to discussion of aberrations within the force. The force encourages officers to come forward with information about corrupt or questionable practices. Although encouragement doesn't always penetrate the blue code, it does create an open environment so that *if* an officer feels like he has something to tell, he has somewhere to go to. Internal Affairs units are proactive in trying to uncover unethical practices and do not sit back and wait for the complaints to come in.

DRUG TESTING OF EMPLOYEES

The greatest lure of corruption is money, no question. But, what about those officers who see their position as one that allows them easy access to the criminal world? Officers confiscate drugs and know where the drug dealers can be found. It is not uncommon to find police officers with substance abuse problems. If an officer does have a drug problem, you can guarantee that they will be far more susceptible to corrupt practices.

Recognizing drug abuse as a gateway to corruption encourages police departments to have comprehensive drug testing procedures. All new applicants are screened. Following hiring, officers can be drug tested randomly, when they exhibit changes in job performance, or when they are involved in a use of force or an on-the-job injury.

Drug abuse is a protected handicap under the Federal Rehabilitation Act of 1973. For this reason, departments offer drug treatment and counseling to those officers who test positive for a drug problem. Efforts are made to assist the officers with their problem prior to any move toward termination or demotion.

WOMEN AND MINORITIES IN POLICING

Gone are the days when police forces were made up of all white men. Now, through better recruiting and fair hiring practices, more minorities and women are joining the U.S. police forces. Although there has been an increase in minority numbers, women are still far underrepresented in police departments.

The first female law enforcement officers were hired in 1845 by the New York City Police Department, however, they worked specifically with female prisoners, or in low level prisons. Since that time opportunities for women have expanded and many women have chosen law enforcement as a career path. This isn't to say the path is without difficulty. Although women constitute approximately half of the work force, the percentage of law enforcement officers that are female has held around 12-15% over the past decade. There are many possible reasons for this phenomenon. For example, nearly all law enforcement agencies require entry level fitness tests which can be inherently favorable to male applicants (the tests are based on percentiles determined by rankings of male abilities). However, despite the fact that women do not have the same natural strength that men do, they are involved in significantly fewer citizen complaints.

When it came to the attention of states across the country that racial minorities were not only less likely to be hired than their white counterparts, but also far less likely to be promoted, it worried officials at the top. Recruiting practices immediately changed to encourage minorities to apply. Hiring practices also changed. Some departments strive to hire a certain percentage of racial minorities to ensure that their departments remain diverse. Also, promotional boards and standards changed to ensure that minorities were getting equal chances when it came time for raises and promotions.

All of this insurance, however, has not done much to increase the number of women in policing. Some research has shown that female police officers are less likely to feel satisfied in their job. What is unclear is why. It could be due to the male exclusivity in the macho field. Researchers have said that if a woman has children it decreases the likelihood that she will be satisfied in the law enforcement field. In an effort to build camaraderie, many professional organizations and local groups of female officers have been created to form a peer-support system.

The first black officer was appointed to the New York City Police Department in 1883. Since the Civil Rights Act of 1954, that number has expanded due to the fact that racial discrimination in hiring practices is prohibited. Despite this fact, it is approximated that they constitute only 11% of law enforcement officers in the United States. This prompts some to believe that discrimination still occurs – whether purposefully or unwittingly. However, agencies are dedicated to ensuring fair hiring practices

POLICE DISCRETION

One of the greatest strengths and simultaneously one of the greatest potentials for abuse within police forces is discretion. **Discretion** is the power of choice exercised by law enforcement personnel in the carrying out of their duties. For instance, we all know that not everyone pulled over for speeding gets a ticket. Sometimes an officer uses his discretion in determining whether to cite a speeding driver.

While departmental policy or statute may dictate what a crime is and how each one should be enforced, police discretion is the ultimate deciding factor in how these situations are handled. Most often, police officers decide against a very strict application of the law, choosing instead to handle many situations in an informal manner.

There are various reasons that discretion exists. Although it might be fairer to just require all officers to enforce all law violations at all times, it would put an incredible strain on the system and while the officer was frantically writing speeding tickets, he could miss a kidnapping. Another reason for discretion is to allow police to make those judgment calls so that the courts don't have to. For instance, if a speeding vehicle is pulled over and the officer finds that the driver is on his way to the hospital to see his child born; and, to make it even worse, the driver is the driver's education teacher at the local high school, it may just be better for everyone involved if he gets off with a stern warning.

Of course the preceding example was extreme, but it is in the best interests of the people of the community, the police department, and the criminal justice system if officers have the ability to practice discretion.

With this great power, however, comes the potential for abuse and it is easy to see where discretion could be used in a counterproductive manner if placed in the wrong hands. Unlike any other job, law enforcement grants its employees great power, the ability to work alone, and puts the safety of others in their hands. This is a potential recipe for corruption and while administrators know this, they also know that with quality controls, discretion is a far more positive aspect than it is negative.

Discussing discretion brings to mind the obvious question of "What determines an officer's use of discretion?" Through research, several factors have been shown to determine an officer's discretionary application of his duties.

What Determines an Officer's Use of Discretion?

1. <u>Departmental Policy and Administration</u>: While discretion is the divergence from policy, policy does influence an officer's use of discretion. For instance, if a force is extremely legalistic and focused on the law enforcement goal of policing, their officers may practice discretion in a more limited manner.

2. <u>Officer's Background</u>: Similar to any job, police employees bring all of their past experience on the job with them. Attitudes, opinions, and even stereotypes will influence an officer's application of the law.

3. <u>Suspect Characteristics</u>: How a suspect appears, his behavior, and attitude will all affect how an officer uses discretion either in his favor or against him.

4. <u>Public Interest</u>: How the community feels about certain crimes will always affect the application of the law. For instance, if a community has problems with speeders on a particular road, officers will come down harder on speeding motorists in an effort to please the community.

5. <u>Approval of the Law</u>: Sometimes laws are passed that the community and the police don't particularly agree with. Many of these crimes are considered "victimless." Examples would be marijuana usage or gambling. When these crimes do not cause alarm in the community, they don't typically warrant much attention from the police.

6. <u>Victims</u>: Often, victims of crime will be quite vocal about their wishes or concerns about particular laws or people. This attention will affect police discretion.

POLICING PRACTICES

Gone are the days of the "hue and cry" and the rattle watch. Crime has changed and law enforcement practices have changed with it. How officers enforce the law and carry out the goals of the police directly affect how effective they are at it.

STYLES OF POLICING

The difference in policing styles from officer to officer and from department to department is often apparent. Different styles work better in different communities and under different circumstances. These styles have evolved through many years of trial and error and while some departments utilize one or the other, the majority of effective departments combine the positive attributes of many styles.

LEGALISTIC

The legalistic style of policing is one that goes "by the book." These departments do not leave much up to discretion. If an offense is against the law, it is treated as such. This means no "warnings" for traffic violations and no leeway for speeders. While legalistic officers and departments may crack down on law violations, they have quite the opposite approach to situations that may warrant their involvement but do not constitute law violations.

For instance, a legalistic officer may not get involved in an argument between neighbors if it has not escalated to a criminal situation. However, if one of the parties breaks the law, the legalistic officer will be there with handcuffs ready. This sort of reactive policing does not successfully fulfill the peacekeeping role of law enforcement and is really only concerned with enforcing the laws.

WATCHMAN

This style is very similar to the legalistic approach in that officers practicing the watchman style have a strong grasp on what is considered criminal. Different from legalistic styles, however, is that watchman police utilize discretion, sometimes to an extreme. Maintaining order is high on the list of priorities for these police officers. They will use methods other than arrests and citations to enforce the law. They may use threats, coercion and sometimes force.

This style of policing is far more common in low income and high crime neighborhoods where officers believe that this informal method may have better results *and* where they believe they can get away with less structured policing styles.

SERVICE

Officers utilizing the service style of policing are very in tune with the communities they serve. They see themselves as cooperative partners in the community, there to provide assistance as well as regulate the law. These departments will be more than willing to work together with social service organizations within the community and prosecutors as well.

They may focus on alternatives to arrest and preventing crime through strong community support. This style of policing is found predominately within upper class neighborhoods where occupants and police alike are educated and well paid.

POLICE-COMMUNITY INTERACTION

While watchman style policing may have been the earliest, followed by the legalistic, administrators began to take a look at the changing face of crime and address community-police relations. It became obvious in the late 1950s and 1960s that law enforcement that only focused on enforcement wasn't enough. The people had to trust the police, to a certain extent, in order for the police to be successful. The police began to look at ways to involve the community in their activities and interact with its people. It was determined that citizens wanted to feel that their concerns were being heard by the police. It was during these early days that some larger cities opened small offices in communities designed solely to create better interaction. The police wanted the communities to feel that they could approach them with complaints and concerns and not worry about retribution. They began to focus on eliminating the fear of the police.

Through neighborhood watch programs, victim assistance programs, and drug awareness education, the police hoped to improve on their reputation. One common problem with maintaining the effectiveness of these programs is that often, the police only offer them where there is already a high level of community satisfaction. Without the police making an attempt to reach out to the high-crime and low-income neighborhoods, little improvement can be made in those areas.

COMMUNITY POLICING

The emphasis on interaction between the police and the communities they serve led to the development of community policing. While initially the move toward community policing was motivated by a selfish need to improve an image, it later became apparent that administrators and police officers truly did care about the communities they served and wanted to be a respected part of them, not only for the sake of effective law enforcement but also for the sake of the safety and happiness of the people.

Community policing can be defined as a cooperative effort between the community and the police to identify criminal problems within the community and search for solutions to those problems in order to enhance their quality of life. Community policing is also heavy on prevention and proactive actions.

By creating an effective partnership between the community and the police, a relationship that was previously strained can turn into one that is forged with a common goal. This allows the community to have a role in the safety of the neighborhoods and a role in the community's satisfaction with the police.

It can be difficult initially for a relationship such as this one to form, particularly in neighborhoods marked by distrust of the police. Often a cooperative effort like this can't be reached without the community members first getting fed up with the crime and lawlessness on their streets. Once the members of the community realize that the police depend on them to function effectively, they are more willing to open up to a potential relationship.

There are several marked differences between a traditional force and a community police force. For instance, a traditional force defines professionalism as a quick response to crime, while a community oriented department defines it as staying close to the community. A traditional force views service-related calls as a hindrance only to be dealt with if there is nothing else to do, while community forces recognize them as a great opportunity to gain respect within the neighborhood.

Another key difference between community-oriented policing and traditional forces is the inclusion of other branches of the criminal justice system. Not only does community policing get the community involved but it also seeks to have involvement from the prosecutor, judiciary, and treatment and prevention programs. The idea of a **community criminal justice** system is modeled after the success of community policing and is taking hold in cities across the nation.

Community policing recognizes the need for cooperation in keeping the citizens satisfied with the police role. Of course the community wants criminals off the streets. But, if programs can work to show the community that they *care* about what happens to people and don't just want to lock everyone up, then they will gain additional respect. By involving prosecutors in actions that benefit the community rather than just getting another conviction under their belt, they will show the community that while crime needs to be dealt with, sometimes there are worthwhile alternatives that can serve the individual and the community better.

In an effort to continue the development of community policing, the Public Safety Partnership and Community Policing Act of 1994 grants funds to agencies who are furthering the community-police partnership. The goal of the act was to encourage officers and their administration to continue proactive policing through constructive community relations.

This important Act had four main purposes:

1. Increase the number of officers directly communicating with the community
2. Provide additional comprehensive training to officers on the fundamentals of community policing
3. Develop programs geared toward allowing the members of the community to act with police in crime prevention
4. Encourage the use of new technology designed to assist in further proactive policing

Community policing has proven to be effective especially in communities that *already* had trust in the police. The real challenge is gaining the trust of people who have always lived in communities with a "we vs. them" mentality. Once the people learn they can trust the local law enforcement they may see the benefits of a cooperative relationship. However, these communities are where the challenge will always lie.

 Legal Aspects of Policing

Up until the 1960s, an individual's Constitutional rights were given little thought by the police and the criminal justice system. It was quite common for the police to abuse their power because no one held them accountable. What they were doing had always worked and no one questioned it. This meant that interrogations often turned violent and warrants were seldom used.

With the civil unrest and attention to human rights that the 1960s brought, however, came another look at individuals' rights. Now you cannot come in contact with the police without their constant attention to those rights being apparent.

There are several Constitutional rights that law enforcement must be careful to protect. Many of them are obviously specific to police duties, while some are applicable to the criminal justice process as a whole. These individual rights are mostly confined to the first ten amendments, also known as the **Bill of Rights**.

Amendment	Guaranteed Right
Fourth	• To be free from **unreasonable searches and seizures** • To be free from **arrest without probable cause**
Fifth	• Protection against **self-incrimination** • Protection from **double-jeopardy** • Right to **Due Process** of law (also in 16th amendment)
Sixth	• Right to a speedy trial • Right to know the charges against you • Right to cross-examine witnesses • Right to an attorney • Right to compel witnesses on your behalf
Eighth	• Protection against excessive fines • Right to reasonable bail • Protection against cruel and unusual punishment

While the Bill of Rights and Constitution provide the individual rights we are all entitled to, the Supreme Court has interpreted these rights and instructed the criminal justice system on how to apply them.

WARREN COURT

Under the leadership of Chief Justice Earl Warren in the 1960s, the Supreme Court made several key decisions in the protection of individual rights. The Court made changes in the areas of arrests, interrogations, and investigation practices. One of the most important achievements of the Court at this time was interpreting the 14th Amendment and establishing that all lower courts and criminal justice entities look to the decisions of the Supreme Court for direction in interpretation of the laws.

This era known as the **"Warren Court"** was marked by multiple important rulings in the criminal justice process. This tightening of the system in an effort to protect individual rights brought with it the understanding that some guilty people would go free with all of the restrictions placed on law enforcement and the courts. However, the Court decided that this would be in the best interest of the people in its primary goal of upholding the individual rights of the people.

DUE PROCESS

One of the cornerstones of individual rights in the face of criminal suspicion and prosecution is due process rights. **Due process** is a broad term that simply means we are entitled to have our individual rights protected at all stages of the criminal justice process. When people say they have a "right to due process," it simply means they have a right to certain protections under the law. This protection is relevant to several areas including at the investigation stage, arrest, and interrogation. Of course, each of these areas has been clarified through a series of landmark Supreme Court Decisions, but the basis for due process is found in the 5th, 6th, and 14th amendments.

Due process is separated into two divisions that coincide with two types of law. **Substantive due process** refers to the creation and definition of what a person's rights are, while **procedural due process** refers to the enforcement of the laws and the punishments for violations. The Constitution's definition of due process is mostly procedural. It dictates procedures that the criminal justice system can and cannot go through when trying to remove a person's rights (for example: arrest and a person's right to remain silent).

Substantive due process is a little stickier and involves those rights that all people are entitled to that may or may not be written out but are accepted universally. It also states that sometimes the government cannot take away someone's rights no matter *how* they do it; they must have substantial *reason* to do it. For instance, the right to privacy is not explicitly stated in the U.S. Constitution, but it is widely accepted as a human right and has been ruled as such through years of case law. The application of substantive due process when dealing with the right to privacy would cause the justice system to veer off from what is known to be right due to precedence and case law, which was largely based on the universally accepted notion that people are entitled to privacy, although it is not a right written in the Constitution.

PRECEDENCE

Before examining Supreme Court decisions it is vital to have a thorough understanding of how precedence works in the United States. **Precedence**, also referred to case law or *stare decisis*, is the principle that ensures prior court decision are considered and incorporated into future similar cases. *Stare decisis* actually means to "let the decision stand." This means that if a judge in Minnesota is ruling on a case with similar circumstances as a well known and respected one in New Jersey, the Minnesotan judge will take into consideration how the judge ruled in New Jersey when making his decision.

Lower courts always look to rulings made by higher courts when making decisions. So, your local court will consider what has been affirmed in the courts of appeals and district courts. They will also look at decisions that have been overturned and avoid the same mistakes. However, "peer courts" may also take into consideration how judges at their level rule. So a judge in one judicial district may look at the neighboring district judge's rulings and consider them. This, of course, does not carry as much weight as higher court decisions.

When the Supreme Court rules on a case, however, it sets precedence for the entire country. The Supreme Court establishes the law of the land with their rulings. If a judge rules contrary to Supreme Court decisions, his cases can and will be overturned on appeal. The Supreme Court has final say in the interpretation and application of law in the criminal justice system.

RULES OF EVIDENCE

The laws and regulations which govern the collection of evidence are extensive; however, they are created to protect the rights of individuals. Evidence which is allowable in court is termed admissible evidence, while things that are not acceptable as evidence are termed inadmissible. In order for something to be admissible in court a set of conditions must be met: relevancy, competency and materiality.

Relevancy refers to information that describes the nature of the case in general, or provides specific facts. Relevant evidence can include a murder weapon, witnesses who sold the murder weapon or witnessed the accused making threats, or documents which demonstrate that tax fraud was in fact occurring (as the case may be). Materiality refers to the fact that the evidence must be important to the case. For example, in a case where a person is on trial for mugging someone, what the suspect was wearing that day may be relevant information (it could identify them as the guilty party); however, the color of the bedspread is likely irrelevant. Competency relates to the reliability of a piece of evidence.

One of the most important forms of inadmissible evidence is referred to as hearsay. This describes information provided by individuals without direct knowledge. A person who heard rumors, or heard the story from a friend of a friend, for example, would not be admissible as a witness because their testimony derives from hearsay.

There are four general characterizations of admissible evidence: real, demonstrative, documentary, and testimonial. Real evidence is physical objects that are involved in the case such as weapons, cars, fingerprints, gunpowder, etc. Demonstrative evidence is illustrations that demonstrate facts about the case, such as maps or photographs of the crime scene. Documentary evidence takes the form of written documents, such as financial records, letters, or newspapers. Finally, testimonial evidence takes the form of oral or written evidence from victims, suspects or witnesses. Testimonial evidence is also referred to as anecdotal evidence.

Apart from problems with relevancy, materiality and competency, evidence may also be inadmissible if it is collected illegally. This occurs can occur if an officer did not have a search warrant when they collected the evidence, or if they violated the terms of the search warrant. If a person was unlawfully arrested and then accused of a crime based on evidence found in their car, it would be inadmissible because it was found illegally. Stolen items are also illegal evidence.

LEGALITIES REGARDING SEARCH AND SEIZURE

The term search and seizure refers to the first stage of the criminal justice process, the stage of investigations and evidence procedures. In the Bill of Rights, this stage of the process is related to the 4th Amendment and the guarantee against unreasonable searches and seizures. Through Supreme Court cases, this Amendment has been further interpreted into rules of evidence and search procedures.

Weeks v. U.S. (1914)

In 1914 the Supreme Court ruled on **Weeks v. U.S.** forming the basis of the **exclusionary rule**. The exclusionary rule states that incriminating evidence must be seized in accordance with the constitutional elements of due process. It also states that if evidence is not seized in accordance with the protections afforded by the Constitution, it will not be considered admissible in court.

Freemont Weeks was accused of using the U.S. mail to sell lottery tickets. In a search of his home, federal officers, without a warrant, seized evidence of the crime as well as personal belongings. In court, Weeks got his personal property returned to him since it was seized illegally. Weeks was convicted of the federal offense and sentenced to federal prison. Through the appeals process, the case ended up at the Supreme Court where it was ruled that the evidence that warranted the conviction was also seized illegally and the conviction was overturned.

Although this case allowed for a guilty criminal to be freed, it was considered worth it in the bigger picture, i.e., the protection of citizens' rights. It is important to note that Weeks could have been re-tried on the case had there been enough evidence to get another conviction. This would not be an instance of double-jeopardy because the appeals court reversed the decision, essentially making it as if there were no prior conviction.

Double jeopardy applies only if a decision has been reached by the courts. For instance, if Weeks had been acquitted in the initial case, a new trial could not be held unless that acquittal was overturned on appeal. If a decision (or ruling) has been made in a case, then another trial cannot be held. Protection against double jeopardy ensures that if an accused defendant is freed by acquittal the prosecution cannot keep "trying" for a conviction, if all facts of the case remain the same.

Silverthorne Lumber Co. v. U.S. (1920)

In 1918 owners of the Silverthorne Lumber Company were accused of failing to pay federal taxes on their company. They were asked to turn over their financial records for investigation and refused, citing their right against self-incrimination (5th Amendment). Federal law enforcement seized their records anyway, without a warrant. In court, the defense for the Lumber Company asked that the illegally seized records be returned to the company, which they were. However, later in the trial, the prosecution presented photocopies of the records as evidence and the Silverthornes were convicted.

Through appeal, the case came before the U.S. Supreme Court in 1920 and the Court ruled in favor of the defendants. What is now known as the **fruit of the poisoned tree doctrine**, the Court ruled that just like illegally seized evidence is not admissible in court, neither is evidence *derived* from illegally seized evidence. Because of the far reaching nature of this ruling, complex cases that are based on one piece of illegally seized evidence can be ruined because of the initial seizure.

Mapp v. Ohio (1961)

Prior to 1961, the exclusionary rule only applied to federal law enforcement, as did the fruit of the poisoned tree doctrine. It was through the case of Mapp v. Ohio that it became applicable to all law enforcement throughout the country. Under the Warren

Court, this decision began a move to ensure that individual rights would be protected at all levels and all stages of the criminal justice process.

Dolree Mapp was suspected of harboring a fugitive. During the investigation, officers came to her door demanding to be allowed to enter. Ms. Mapp refused and the officers forced their way in regardless, without a warrant. Upon entering and searching the home the officers arrested Mapp for being in possession of pornographic materials. She was convicted of this charge but took the appeal all the way to the Supreme Court. It was the Warren Court justices who looked at Mapp's case and saw that there was a divergence from the intention of the law if only federal law enforcement officers were held to the standards outlined in prior evidence gathering rules. Under the 14th Amendment it was determined that those standards must be adhered to by all law enforcement in order to keep individual rights protected.

Chimel v. California (1969)

Another Warren Court decision, Chimel v. California was vital in defining the scope of legal searches when no search warrant was present. Mr. Chimel was arrested at his home by local law enforcement on an *arrest* warrant stating he was suspected of burglarizing a coin shop. Upon his arrest his entire home, attic, and garage were searched without a search warrant. Evidence was uncovered in his garage that was used in gaining his conviction.

The Supreme Court ruled that the areas that can be searched while performing an arrest are limited without the presence of a search warrant. Officers can search the person being arrested and those areas within reach of the defendant to protect themselves, prevent escape, and prevent the destruction of evidence. This type of search is referred to as a **search incident to arrest**. However, when the search goes beyond the reach of the defendant or is for no valid reason, it is not permissible without an additional search warrant or without the consent of the person whose property is being searched.

While it is commonly said that a man's home is his castle, evidentiary rules are created to protect the people, not the homes or structures they occupy. What this means is that a homeless person has a right to protection from unreasonable searches and seizures even if the place in question is a box. The standard used when applying these laws is where a person has a reasonable "expectation of privacy" for the area in question.

U.S. v. Leon (1984)

Moving into a new era of the Supreme Court, under Chief Justice Warren E. Burger, the Court started making exceptions to the evidentiary rules laid out previously.

In the case of U.S. v. Leon, Leon was suspected of drug trafficking and police obtained a search warrant. When a search warrant is applied for, an affidavit must display that probable cause exists for the suspected offenses. A magistrate signed the warrant in this case and Leon was later arrested and convicted for drug trafficking because of the evidence that was seized in executing the warrant. Through appeals it was determined that the original affidavit requesting the warrant failed to show sufficient probable cause and the warrant should not have been issued.

The question posed to the Supreme Court was whether evidence seized by officers acting "in good faith" could be admitted in Court. The officers in this situation had every reason to believe that they were fulfilling a legitimate warrant and that they were collecting evidence in the legally required manner.

In what has become known as the **good faith exception to the exclusionary rule**, the Supreme Court ruled in favor of the State and Leon's conviction was upheld.

ADDITIONAL EXCEPTIONS

Modifications and exceptions to the exclusionary rule continued with *Maryland v. Garrison (1987)*, which ruled that evidence was admissible even if the information on the warrant was incorrect. This case involved an apartment search in which the warrant specified the entire 3rd floor of a building. It was later discovered that the 3rd floor included multiple apartments that shouldn't have been included in the search.

In the 1990 case of *Illinois v. Rodriguez*, the Supreme Court ruled that if the police had a reasonable belief that a person had the right to consent to a search, they could legally search. This came about when a woman accused a man of assault. She told police that she lived with the man and unlocked the apartment door so they could search. Later it was found that Rodriguez no longer lived there and did not have authority to grant the search. Because the officers had a reasonable belief that the search was legal, however, the fruits of the search were upheld.

PLAIN VIEW

The **plain view doctrine** is one that was first addressed in the case of *Harris v. U.S. (1968)*, where an officer was processing an impounded vehicle and came across evidence from a robbery. The plain view doctrine states that anything that falls into the "plain view" of an officer who is legally entitled to be in that position to have said view, is subject to seizure and can be introduced as evidence.

This doctrine is often used when police are responding to accidents or emergencies. For instance, if a police officer responding to an accident finds cocaine on the front seat of one of the vehicles, he can confiscate the evidence and place the owner under arrest if the owner can be determined.

However, if the officer is not entitled to be in the position they are in when they see the evidence in question, it cannot be taken and introduced as evidence. Also, the evidence has to be in plain view. The officer cannot go digging through the person's possessions to uncover incriminating evidence because it would not have been considered to be in plain view.

Of course, since the case of Harris v. U.S. established the doctrine, other cases have come along that further interpreted and restricted it. In the case of ***U.S. v. Irizarry (1982)***, it was decided at the Circuit Court level that officers can't move objects out of the way to bring evidence into plain view.

Arizona v. Hicks (1987) also reiterated the plain view doctrine when the U.S. Supreme Court didn't allow evidence that had been uncovered by moving a stereo. Upholding the plain view doctrine, the Court has ruled on several cases regarding what is considered "plain view."

VEHICLE SEARCHES

Vehicles present interesting problems for law enforcement. They are obviously very mobile and can conceal many things. They often have unique laws and precedents created just for applications related to them.

In 1964 a man named Preston was arrested and taken to jail for vagrancy. His car was impounded and the police then searched it for contraband, and discovered two guns. He was charged for the weapons and appealed his conviction to the Supreme Court. In ***Preston v. U.S. (1964)*** the Court found that because the vehicle was secure and in police custody, they had no reason to search it for contraband. Had the police really wanted to search the vehicle they could have obtained a warrant.

Later in ***South Dakota v. Opperman (1976)***, it was ruled that the police *could* search a vehicle for the purposes of inventorying property while it was impounded. If they discovered illegal substances under these circumstances, their seizure would hold up in court. This was even true when referring to items found inside containers within the vehicle, as long as it was when processing inventory that the vehicle was searched. ***Colorado v. Bertine (1987)*** affirmed this. In the contrary case ***Florida v. Wells (1990)***, the court agreed with a lower court that suppressed evidence (marijuana) found within a locked suitcase in the trunk of a vehicle being inventoried. Apparently police could not tamper with locking devices solely for the inventory of property when there was no warrant for a search specifically geared to finding illegal items or substances.

Similar to searches done while inventorying property are searches done with the consent of the vehicle's owner. No warrant is needed if the owner of a vehicle consents to a search. In ***Florida v. Jiminez (1991)***, it was determined that if a person grants permission to officers for the searching of his vehicle, the consent is implied to mean all reasonable areas of the vehicle. In this case the owner consented to the search and a large amount of cocaine was discovered in a bag on the floor. Throughout the appeals process the defendant claimed that when he consented to the search he did not consent to the officer's opening the bag. The Court sided with the officers, interpreting the consent as including the contents of the bag.

What is included in the areas of a vehicle to be searched has been the topic of many constitutional debates. The most recent standard, and one that will continue to be used, states that when probable cause exists to justify the search of a vehicle, then it justifies the search of the entire vehicle. In **United States v. Ross (1982)**, the Court sided with police when determining that they were not outside the legal scope of the search when they discovered a bag in the trunk containing heroin.

Another issue concerning searches and vehicles is searches incident to arrest when the suspect is in a vehicle. Keeping in mind the purpose of searches incident to arrest, the Court has held that these types of searches, when involving a vehicle, are to only include the areas of the vehicle immediately accessible to the arrestee. Therefore, if there is no additional probable cause or search warrant, and an arrest warrant is being served on a driver or passenger of the vehicle, the trunk most likely cannot be searched.

As you can see, vehicle searches are sticky areas with several precedents of importance. Officers must be incredibly savvy when conducting searches of vehicles and the contents within. They must know the ins and outs of the laws relating to searches of vehicles or risk seeing a case get thrown out due to the exclusionary rule or fruits of the poisonous tree doctrine.

EMERGENCY EXCEPTIONS

It is important to note that there are some situations that are considered emergency searches and are justifiable due to some immediate need concerning either:

1. public safety;
2. the potential escape of a dangerous suspect; or
3. the loss or destruction of evidence.

Any one of those situations can allow an exception to the Fourth Amendment's requirement of a warrant. Several cases have upheld these emergency circumstances including the 1967 case of **Warden v. Hayden** in which a home was searched following a report of an armed robber in the building. Another case upholding these exceptions was **Maryland v. Buie (1990)**, which allowed for the searching of premises where a dangerous person may be hiding.

LEGALITIES REGARDING ARRESTS

The seizure of a person is known as an arrest and this type of seizure is also very tightly regulated and controlled. Knowing when an arrest has occurred may be tricky. An **arrest** is when the police limit a person's ability to leave. There may be no handcuffs, no Miranda rights read, and no "You're under arrest" muttered. Often, a person knows they have been placed under arrest only when they try to leave. This "freedom to leave" standard has been upheld by the courts on many occasions and seems to be the ultimate test in determining if a seizure has taken place. Probable cause is the minimum requirement for an arrest to be made. If an officer has probable cause that a person committed a crime, he can prohibit the individual from leaving.

Typically, arrests happen after questioning. An officer will question a subject to develop probable cause and then can restrain the suspect's movements. Sometimes arrests are made when a crime is discovered "in progress." Also, the obvious arrests are those that are committed through the use of an arrest warrant. The majority of states allow for the arrest of a suspect based on probable cause but in some situations a warrant is required.

SEARCH INCIDENT TO ARREST

As discussed earlier: "The Supreme Court ruled that the areas that can be searched while performing an arrest are limited without the presence of a search warrant. Officers can search the person being arrested and those areas within reach of the defendant to protect themselves, prevent escape, and prevent the destruction of evidence." This is referred to as a search incident to arrest.

This evidentiary rule became clarified through several cases beginning with ***Chimel v. California (1969)***. Again in ***Robinson v. U.S. (1973)***, the Court upheld the search incident to arrest when a police officer was making an arrest for driving without a license, and searched the vehicle to ensure he was in no danger (looking for weapons). What he found was heroin and the suspect was charged and later convicted. Because the officer's safety was being protected through his search, the evidence (heroin) was admissible in court.

The well known case of ***Terry v. Ohio (1968)*** guaranteed an officer's right to "stop and frisk" individuals when they are ensuring their safety. The Terry case did not require probable cause and instead stated that officers have a right to protect themselves and frisking someone should be allowed. Police still refer to this type of search as a "Terry stop." This is often used when officers are in the field interviewing and investigating. Because officers conducting a stop and frisk are doing so to protect themselves, not just any evidence can be seized through this type of search.

If an officer is doing a pat down and discovers something in the pocket of the individual but knows it is not a weapon, they cannot arrest the person for what they have, whether it be cocaine or counterfeit money. This would defeat the intent of the law. ***Minnesota v. Dickerson (1993)*** affirmed this when it stated that cocaine found in the pocket of a stop and frisk subject was not admissible because the officer knew from "plain touch" that the cocaine was not a weapon and the purpose of that type of search is only to uncover weapons.

Further fine-tuning the times when a person can be detained was the case of ***Brown v. Texas (1979)*** where two officers stopped Brown and asked him for identification. Brown refused and was cited. It was later determined that the police didn't think he was dangerous nor did they believe he had committed or was going to commit a crime. They just wanted to know his identity. The charges against Brown were overturned and it was determined that a person cannot be punished or detained for refusal to show identification.

In the case of ***Smith v. Ohio (1990)***, the Supreme Court held that a citizen has a right to protect their property from unsubstantiated police search. This came about when Smith was walking down the street carrying a brown paper sack. Police officers asked to look in the bag (having no probable cause) and Smith denied them this. The police found marijuana in the bag and Smith was arrested. The Court held that Smith was not posing a risk nor was there any reason for the police to stop him. They stated that a person walking down the street with his possessions in a paper sack had as great an expectation of privacy as one who was walking with illegal documents in his leather briefcase.

In a conflicting opinion, the case of ***California v. Hodari (1991)*** held that suspects fleeing from the police who throw evidence as they retreat, may be charged based on the abandoned evidence. This case involved two youths who were approached by officers and ran. As they ran, one tossed a crack rock that was later retrieved by the officers. Because the officers did not attempt to "stop" the juveniles and there was no "seizure" (the officers didn't even ask the juveniles to stop running), the evidence was not seized illegally in the execution of an arrest or "stop and frisk."

EMERGENCY SEARCHES OF PEOPLE

Similar to emergency situations in regards to searches of property, there are emergency situations that warrant the searches of persons. For example, if a person strongly resembles a description of an armed bank robber, a police officer would be entitled to search the person in assurance that he wasn't armed. Similarly, people may be searched for reasons that save lives or prevent the fleeing of dangerous suspects or destruction of evidence.

In recognition of these emergency situations, the Supreme Court ruled in *Arkansas v. Sanders (1979)* that these types of emergency searches were constitutional when the cost of obtaining a warrant would cause a danger to the police or a possible loss of evidence. In other words, if in the course of time it would take to obtain the warrant, one of these unwanted situations would arise, an emergency exists and the search can be performed.

In a more extreme version of an emergency situation, Borchadt, a federal inmate, was suspected of a heroin overdose. He was transported to a hospital where his heart stopped and he had to be revived. He was given a dosage of a counteracting drug and regained consciousness. The hospital wanted to pump his stomach, to which he refused. However, he ended up vomiting several bags of heroin. These bags were used in his prosecution despite his refusal to consent to the search of his body. In *Borchadt v. U.S. (1987)*, the appeals court affirmed that the emergency situation of the defendant's health outweighed his objections to the search.

LEGALITIES REGARDING INTERROGATION

Interrogations are another area where procedure has been fine-tuned through years of trial and error. Several cases have gone to the Supreme Court where they have clarified how the laws are to be applied in reference to interrogations.

Brown v. Mississippi (1936)

An **interrogation** is when the police act in an information gathering capacity by interviewing suspects. In the first major case surrounding interrogations, *Brown v. Mississippi (1936)*, a store owner was killed in the commission of a robbery. The storekeeper was white and the suspect was black. Immediately following the murder a posse formed and went about lynching the suspect, repeatedly hanging him and letting him down, waiting for a confession. When this didn't work, they moved onto other suspects trying the same method. One person finally confessed and the remaining suspects were whipped until they "confessed" as well. Three men were convicted of the murder of the store owner and their convictions were upheld on appeal in Mississippi. One of the defendants continued the appeals process to the Supreme Court where the case was finally overturned on the grounds that physical abuse leading to a confession taints the confession.

Ashcraft v. Tennessee (1942)

This case established that "inherent coercion" could also bring about a false confession and therefore was not allowed. Ashcraft was charged with the murder of a family member. He was interrogated through an entire weekend until he finally confessed to the murder on Monday morning. He was not physically abused but faced relentless questioning. His conviction was overturned by the Supreme Court for violating the 5th Amendment protection against self incrimination.

Escobedo v. Illinois (1964)

This case brought about the right to have an attorney present at interrogation. Escobedo was being interrogated for murder and asked to see his lawyer. Police told him this was not possible. His attorney showed up at the station and asked to speak with Escobedo. Police told the attorney that he could see Escobedo after the interrogation was finished. His case was later overturned because of the police's failure to recognize Escobedo's constitutional right to counsel.

In another vitally important case regarding interrogations, it was determined that if an interrogation is being conducted and the suspect requests an attorney, *all* interrogations must immediately stop and the suspect's request be honored. This standard was upheld in the case of **Edwards v. Arizona (1981)**. **Minnick v. Mississippi (1990)** further stated that interrogations cannot resume after the suspect has spoken with the attorney and the attorney has departed.

MIRANDA RIGHTS

Probably the most famous of all Supreme Court cases regarding the criminal process is that of **Miranda v. Arizona (1965)**. Ernesto Miranda was arrested in Phoenix and charged with rape. He was identified by the accuser as the suspect. He was interrogated for only two hours and subsequently signed a confession, which led to his conviction.

However, on appeal his conviction was overturned as unconstitutional because the police failed to inform Miranda of his rights. The Court added that the defendant must be told prior to questioning that he has the right to remain silent, that anything he says can be used against him in court, that he has a right to an attorney and if he can't afford one he will be appointed one. The defendant must have the opportunity to exercise these rights at any stage of the interrogation process. The defendant can waive these rights and answer any questions he chooses, but must be made aware of the rights prior to questioning.

Miranda rights have become such a normal part of police business that almost anyone who watches police television shows or movies can recite the rights. Also, police typically carry the rights written down on a wallet card to ensure they do not miss any points when reciting them.

Initially law enforcement was resistant to the Miranda rights because it put them in a position to enforce as well as educate. They didn't feel they should be responsible for the criminal justice education of suspects. Heavy attacks have been waged against the Miranda decision, but it stands firm.

WAIVING MIRANDA RIGHTS

Miranda rights may only be waived if they are waived knowingly and willingly. This simply means that the suspect must be informed of the rights before he can waive them. This also means that the suspect cannot be coerced into waiving the Miranda rights. Also determined through Supreme Court decisions is the ruling that the defendant must be able to understand what the rights are and the consequences for waiving them.

INEVITABLE DISCOVERY EXCEPTION

As with all rules, there are exceptions and the Miranda rights are no different. The inevitable discovery exception came about after the Warren Court and its emphasis on individual rights. It came during the Burger Court, when the Court was more in tune with the imperfections of legal procedure and the difficulties police had in protecting individual rights at all times.

In the case of *Nix v. Williams (1984)*, Williams was charged and convicted of murder. While in a patrol car, an officer led Williams to a confession and his leading the police to the victim's body. His Miranda rights had been read to him previously but he was not reminded of his right to counsel prior to the officer questioning him. His original conviction was overturned and his confession ruled inadmissible.

However, he was tried again and convicted again. Although the confession was not used in the second trial, the discovery of the victim's body was. The case again was appealed, this time to the Supreme Court who ruled in favor of the State saying that the body would have been discovered without the confession; that it was an "inevitable discovery."

PUBLIC SAFETY EXCEPTION

Yet another exception to the rule is what is known as the public safety exception. This exception came about with the decision of *New York v. Quarles (1984)*. Quarles was convicted of rape but sought to have the conviction overturned because he had not been advised of his rights prior to the police asking him one question, "Where is your gun?" The police followed Quarles into an A&P store after being told by his accuser that he had gone in there with a gun. Upon finding Quarles and seeing his holster empty, the officer, fearing for the safety of those around, asked the now infamous question. The Supreme Court sided with the officer in this case, stating that issues of public safety overrode the need for Miranda rights when it came to this singular question.

Another public safety exception to the Miranda rights was in the case of *Colorado v. Connelly (1986)*. Connelly, later determined to be mentally ill, approached officers and wanted to confess to the murder of a child. He was informed of his rights multiple times as he continued on his confession. Later he asserted he was hearing voices and on appeal claimed that he confessed only because the voices told him to. The Court upheld his conviction and stated that "self coercion" did not negate the reading of the rights nor did it constitute coercion on the part of the officers.

OVERVIEW

Although much of what dictates police behavior and action is written into departmental policy, even more of it is governed by already existing precedents from the Courts of the land. Although the police are not explicitly required to obey the decisions of the Supreme Court, they know that if they choose not to, the majority of their cases will be thrown out of court.

The Courts of the land establish the rules by which the police must play and the police recognize that in order to be successful at their roles they must abide by the rules.

 # Sample Test Questions

1) The Code of Hammurabi was created by King Hammurabi of

   A) Israel
   B) Babylon
   C) Sodom
   D) Egypt

The correct answer is B:) Babylon. The Code of Hammurabi was created in ancient Babylon between the years 1700-2250 BC.

2) The principle of Lex talionis originated in:

   A) The Bible
   B) The Code of Hammurabi
   C) The Constitution of the United States
   D) The Justinian Code

The correct answer is B:) The Code of Hammurabi. This Code stressed the principle that no one person was worth more than another.

3) Approximately what percentage of law enforcement officers are African American?

   A) 2%
   B) 6%
   C) 11%
   D) 22%

The correct answer is C:) 11%.

4) Ancient police from this location carried a bat topped with a metal knob similar to police batons seen today.

   A) Babylon
   B) Egypt
   C) Rome
   D) London

The correct answer is B:) Egypt. Little more is known about these early recorded police.

5) Approximately what percentage of all law enforcement jobs are held by women?

   A) 4%
   B) 12%
   C) 24%
   D) 33%

The correct answer is B:) 12%. Many people feel that this is a result of unfair hiring practices that inherently favor male applicants.

6) How were the ancient Greek ephor chosen?

   A) Nomination
   B) Election
   C) They served as punishment for petty crimes
   D) Lottery

The correct answer is B:) Election. Anyone was entitled to run for the position of ephor.

7) Who were the first to separate law into "public" and "private" laws?

   A) Romans
   B) English
   C) Greek
   D) Egyptians

The correct answer is A:) Romans. The Romans first separated law into two divisions.

8) Which early police officers began as firefighters and were then tasked with filling both roles?

   A) Night watchmen
   B) Vigiles urbani
   C) Ephori
   D) Lictors

The correct answer is B:) Vigiles urbani. They began their careers as firefighters and took on a law enforcement role under Augustus.

9) Translated, this term means "watchmen of the city"

   A) Night watchmen
   B) Vigiles urbani
   C) Ephori
   D) Lictors

The correct answer is B:) Vigiles urbani. The police in modern day Italy are often still called by this title.

10) This early group of police were employed by early magistrates

   A) Night watchmen
   B) Vigiles urbani
   C) Ephori
   D) Lictors

The correct answer is D:) Lictors. Lictors were tasked with protecting the magistrates and fulfilling their wishes.

11) What is the term used to describe a group of ten families living in relative proximity in a communal effort to control crime?

   A) Fasces
   B) Reeve
   C) Tithe
   D) None of the above

The correct answer is C:) Tithe. The tithing system was dominant in England following the feudal system.

12) Which victimless crime is the most commonly prosecuted?

   A) Drug related crimes
   B) Prostitution
   C) Gambling
   D) None of the above

The correct answer is A:) Drug related crimes. The Bureau of Justice Statistics reports that just over half of all individuals in prison are there as a result of drug related crimes.

13) The "hue and cry" method required people within close proximity to do what when they heard someone calling out?

   A) Stop what they were doing and go home
   B) Stop what they were doing and get the chief tithingman
   C) Stop what they were doing and assist in the apprehension of a criminal
   D) Provide emergency first aid to the injured victim

The correct answer is C:) Stop what they were doing and assist in the apprehension of a criminal. The tithing system encouraged community cooperation in combating crime.

14) A group of ten tithes is called what?

   A) A shire
   B) A reeve
   C) A vassal
   D) Military district

The correct answer is B:) A reeve. A group of reeves was referred to as a shire.

15) Prostitution is an example of a

   A) Capital crime
   B) Victimless crime
   C) Violent crime
   D) Property crime

The correct answer is B:) Victimless crime. A victimless crime is any crime which does not harm another person or their property, and which does not infringe on the rights of another individual.

16) What group, led by William the Conqueror, invaded England in 1066?

   A) Normans
   B) Franklins
   C) Scottish tribesman
   D) Frankpledges

The correct answer is A:) Normans. William the Conqueror and the Normans came to England and established the Frankpledge system.

17) Translated, what does the term *posse comitatus* mean?

   A) Power of the people
   B) Power of the land
   C) Power in numbers
   D) All for one, one for all

The correct answer is B:) Power of the land. The concept of posse comitatus was a unique power of the shire-reeve.

18) What did the Frankpledge system do in regards to the community cooperation utilized in the tithing system?

   A) Abolished it
   B) Restricted the power of the community
   C) Expanded on it
   D) None of the above

The correct answer is C:) Expanded on it. Under the Frankpledge system, the community continued to serve a vital role.

19) Which Constitutional Amendment ensures due process?

   A) Fifth
   B) Sixth
   C) Fourteenth
   D) Both A and C

The correct answer is D:) Both A and C. The Fifth Amendment is the due process amendment, and the Fourteenth Amendment specifically extends the protections to former slaves.

20) The UCR Program is an effort to

   A) Rank various agencies within the United States government.
   B) Produce reliable and useful statistical information.
   C) Identify areas with ineffective crime fighting strategies.
   D) None of the above.

The correct answer is B:) Produce reliable and useful statistical information. The UCR Program can give valuable information about crime levels and distributions, but should not be used as a ranking system.

21) What did the Leges Henrici do?

   A) Established that some laws needed to be punished by the throne
   B) Outlawed the "hue and cry"
   C) Required citizens to pledge loyalty to the throne
   D) Further defined crimes as being moral sins

The correct answer is A:) Established that some laws needed to be punished by the throne. This distinction further separated public and private laws.

22) What was one major issue with the utilization of thief takers?

   A) Anyone could be a thief taker
   B) They demanded immunity
   C) They were tightly regulated
   D) None of the above

The correct answer is A:) Anyone could be a thief taker. Lack of regulations meant that thief takers were often petty criminals themselves.

23) Which of the following is NOT a reason that a person would chose not to report a crime?

   A) Fear
   B) Emotional trauma
   C) They consider it insignificant
   D) All of the above are reasons that crimes go unreported

The correct answer is D:) All of the above are reasons that crimes go unreported.

24) When was the London Metropolitan Police Force created?

   A) 1834
   B) 1829
   C) 1902
   D) 1865

The correct answer is B:) 1829. The London Metropolitan Police Force was created in 1829 by Sir Robert Peel.

25) In New Amsterdam, the _____ was the first in law enforcement, acting to enforce the laws of the Dutch West India Company.

   A) Burgher watch
   B) Sheriff attorney
   C) Rattle watch
   D) None of the above

The correct answer is B:) Sheriff attorney. The sheriff attorney acted as prosecutor and police.

26) What happened in 1664 that immediately decreased crime in New York City?

   A) The NYC police department was established
   B) Citizens again employed the hue and cry method
   C) Street lights were added
   D) Strict curfews were established

The correct answer is C:) Street lights were added. Prior to 1664 all streets were dark save for lanterns.

27) In 1844 which U.S. city modeled the first modern police force after the London Metropolitan Police?

   A) New York
   B) Boston
   C) Chicago
   D) Charleston

The correct answer is A:) New York. Soon after other major cities followed suit.

28) In 1882, which U.S. city developed the first detective unit?

   A) New York
   B) Boston
   C) Chicago
   D) Charleston

The correct answer is C:) Chicago.

29) Who is known as the "father of law enforcement"?

   A) Henry Fielding
   B) Orlando Wilson
   C) August Vollmer
   D) None of the above

The correct answer is C:) August Vollmer. Vollmer made great strides in the professionalization of law enforcement.

30) Which was created in 1883 in an attempt to reduce corruption?

   A) Pendleton Act
   B) Hamilton Act
   C) Kerner Commission
   D) Knapp Commission

The correct answer is A:) Pendleton Act. This Act was passed by Congress and created the civil service sector.

31) Approximately what percentage of rapes are not reported?

   A) 10%
   B) 33%
   C) 45%
   D) 60%

The correct answer is D:) 60%. Some reasons for this are that victims are too embarrassed or ashamed to admit the crime has occurred. Many are emotionally traumatized and react by ignoring the fact that it occurred.

32) Which of the following warned that we were moving towards a society that was "separate but unequal"?

   A) Pendleton Act
   B) Hamilton Act
   C) Kerner Commission
   D) Knapp Commission

The correct answer is C:) Kerner Commission. The Kerner Commission addressed police brutality and racial tensions.

33) Which of the following are courts that can only hear certain aspects of certain cases?

   A) Courts of appellate jurisdiction
   B) Courts of limited jurisdiction
   C) Courts of general jurisdiction
   D) None of the above

The correct answer is B:) Courts of limited jurisdiction. These courts are the lowest level courts in the state court systems.

34) Which of the following is NOT collected under UCR?

   A) Statistics about hate crimes
   B) Statistics about arson
   C) Statistics relating to sentencing of those convicted
   D) Statistics about theft

The correct answer is C:) Statistics relating to the sentencing of those convicted. The UCR collects data about offenses, not about the findings of a court or jury, or the sentencing of criminals.

35) Which amendments products a person from self-incrimination?

   A) Fourth
   B) Third
   C) Fifth
   D) Fourteenth

The correct answer is C:) Fifth. The Fifth Amendment additionally protects against double jeopardy, and ensures due process.

36) Police Officers must obtain a search warrant to gather evidence due to which Constitutional Amendment?

   A) Fourth
   B) Sixth
   C) Eighth
   D) Fourteenth

The correct answer is A:) Fourth. The Fourth Amendment protects against unreasonable searches and seizures.

37) Which of the following is NOT a protection of the Sixth Amendment?

   A) Right to a speedy and public trial
   B) The accused must know what they are accused of
   C) The accused must be allowed to have witnesses in their favor
   D) Protection against being tried twice for the same crime

The correct answer is D:) Protection against being tried twice for the same crime. This is a protection extended by the Fifth Amendment.

38) A judge would not set bail at 20 million dollars for a person accused of stealing a corn dog because of which constitutional amendment?

   A) Fourth
   B) Sixth
   C) Eighth
   D) Fourteenth

The correct answer is C:) Eighth. The Eighth Amendment protects against excessive bail and cruel and unusual punishments.

39) In order for a crime to have been committed two conditions must be met: mens rea and

   A) Mala in se
   B) Mala prohibita
   C) Habeas corpus
   D) Actus rea

The correct answer is D:) Actus rea. These two Latin phrases stand for guilty mind and guilty action. In other words, a person must have intent as well as have physically committed a crime.

40) Given that most people consider murder to be morally wrong, a person who is guilty of murder has committed which type of crime?

   A) Mala in se
   B) Mala prohibita
   C) Mens rea
   D) Actus rea

The correct answer is A:) Mala in se. This refers to crimes that are just generally accepted to be morally wrong (e.g., murder, theft, rape, etc.). They contrast with Mala prohibita crimes which are just law violations (e.g., speeding).

41) How many district courts are there in the United States?

A) 13
B) 94
C) 6
D) 42

The answer is B:) 94.

42) How long of a term does a federal magistrate serve?

A) Lifetime
B) 4 years
C) 8 years
D) None of the above

The correct answer is C:) 8 years. The magistrates are appointed by the judges, who serve life terms.

43) What type of jurisdiction do Federal circuit courts have?

A) Appellate
B) General
C) Mandatory
D) Limited

The correct answer is C:) Mandatory. Federal circuit courts must hear all cases brought before them.

44) Who confirms a Supreme Court nomination?

A) President
B) Senate
C) U.S. Attorney General
D) Voters in the district of nomination

The correct answer is B:) Senate. The U.S. Senate confirms the President's nomination.

45) Which term refers to the power of the U.S. Supreme Court to address any decision from any court in the nation?

   A) Appellate review
   B) Judicial review
   C) Appellate jurisdiction
   D) General jurisdiction

The correct answer is B:) Judicial review. Judicial review is possibly the greatest power of the Supreme Court.

46) Which of the following are the goals of corrections?

   A) Retribution, incapacitation, correction, reformation
   B) Incapacitation, reformation, coercion, retribution
   C) Rehabilitation, incapacitation, retribution, reformation
   D) None of the above

The correct answer is D:) None of the above. The four goals of corrections are incapacitation, deterrence, retribution, and rehabilitation.

47) Which department does the Secret Service operate under?

   A) Department of Justice
   B) Department of the Treasury
   C) Department of Homeland Security
   D) Department of Security

The correct answer is C:) Department of Homeland Security. This is true although the Secret Service also has many treasury related duties.

48) Which of the following early correctional models required inmates to work in silence all day?

   A) Medical model
   B) Pennsylvania system
   C) Auburn system
   D) None of the above

The correct answer is C:) Auburn system. The Auburn system was created at the Auburn State Prison in New York.

49) Which of the following is used to determine if probable cause exists?

   A) Preponderance of the evidence
   B) Beyond a reasonable doubt
   C) Reasonable belief
   D) Rational occurrence

The correct answer is C:) Reasonable belief. This standard of proof is fairly low when compared with the others listed.

50) Which of the following is would NOT be admissible as evidence?

   A) A map of the crime location which illustrates the feasibility of the crime.
   B) A series of private documents which demonstrate that the suspect was in deep financial trouble.
   C) The murder weapon which was discovered at the scene of the crime.
   D) The testimony of a friend of a neighbor who heard rumors that a couple was constantly fighting.

The correct answer is D:) The testimony of a friend of a neighbor who heard rumors that a couple was constantly fighting. This would be an example of hearsay, which is not admissible as evidence.

51) Which of the following is NOT true of the Knapp Commission?

   A) It was organized to investigate corruption in New York City.
   B) It consisted of a board of five individuals.
   C) It was organized in 1901 by the current governor.
   D) Neither B nor C is true

The correct answer is C:) It was organized in 1901 by the current governor. The Knapp Commission was organized in 1970.

52) Which of the following Constitutional Amendments is NOT specifically related to law enforcement?

   A) Third
   B) Fourth
   C) Fifth
   D) Eighth

The correct answer is A:) Third. The Third Amendment states that citizens can't be forced to house troops during times of peace.

53) Which of the following is not true about plea bargains?

   A) They are controversial
   B) They take power away from the judiciary
   C) They decide the defendant's sentence
   D) They are optional

The correct answer is C:) They decide the defendant's sentence. The plea bargain decides the charge and makes a sentence recommendation, but the judge ultimately decides the sentence.

54) Which of the following are not challenges used in the jury selection process?

   A) Peremptory challenge
   B) Challenge to the affray
   C) Challenge to the array
   D) Challenge for cause

The correct answer is B:) Challenge to the affray. The rest are legitimate challenges used by either the prosecution or defense when dismissing jurors.

55) What is it called when the judge gives instructions to the jury prior to deliberations?

   A) Charge
   B) Deliverance
   C) Impart
   D) None of the above

The correct answer is A:) Charge. The judge's charge is the instructions given to the jury.

56) Who typically completes a pre-sentence investigation?

   A) Prosecutor
   B) Clerk of the court
   C) Probation officer
   D) Arresting officer

The correct answer is C:) Probation officer. Probation officers complete the PSI because of their expertise in offender's success while under community supervision.

57) Which of the following is NOT a responsibility of the Secret Service?

   A) Protecting former Presidents of the United States.
   B) Investigating counterfeiting and money laundering.
   C) Protecting visiting dignitaries to the United States.
   D) All of the above are responsibilities of the Secret Service.

The correct answer is D:) All of the above are responsibilities of the Secret Service. The Secret Service has many protective and treasury related duties.

58) Which of the following sentencing recommendations is a judge required to follow?

   A) From the prosecutor in the case of a plea agreement
   B) From a probation officer in a pre-sentence investigation
   C) Noth A & B
   D) None of the above

The correct answer is D:) None of the above. The judge makes the sentencing decisions independently of recommendations.

59) Which of the following is considered a "self reporting" survey?

   A) UCR
   B) NIBRS
   C) NCVS
   D) Both B & C

The correct answer is C:) NCVS. The National Crime Victimization Survey relies on victim self reporting for crime data.

60) Which term refers to the number of crimes that go unreported?

   A) Blue shadow of crime
   B) Dark figure of crime
   C) Shadow of reported crime
   D) None of the above

The correct answer is B:) Dark figure of crime. These crimes are difficult for typical measures to uncover.

61) What is the "clearance rate"?

   A) Amount of reported crime
   B) Number of arrests cleared by conviction
   C) Number of reported crimes cleared by arrest
   D) Number of crimes uncovered through self-reporting

The correct answer is C:) Number of reported crimes cleared by arrest. The clearance rate is used in compiling data for the UCR.

62) How many U.S. Marshals are there?

   A) 36
   B) 42
   C) 94
   D) 52

The correct answer is C:) 94. There is one U.S. Marshal per federal judicial district.

63) Which Federal law enforcement agency is responsible for the witness protection program?

   A) FBI
   B) U.S. Marshals
   C) ICE
   D) DEA

The correct answer is B:) U.S. Marshals.

64) Which federal law enforcement agency is responsible for the national fingerprint database?

   A) FBI
   B) U.S. Marshals
   C) ICE
   D) DEA

The correct answer is A:) FBI.

65) Which of the following is NOT a side effect of police work on the officer's family relations?

   A) The officer can become cynical and uncommunicative
   B) Crazy schedules resulting in strain in interactions
   C) The officer may die in the line of duty
   D) All of the above can result from police work

The correct answer is D:) All of the above can result from police work.

66) If an officer threatens to give an individual a ticket unless they pay a certain amount of money, it is referred to as which type of police corruption?

   A) Ticket fixing
   B) Police extortion
   C) Bribery
   D) Kickbacks

The correct answer is B:) Police extortion. This is when officers use their position to unlawfully obtain money.

67) An attempt by police to improve interactions with individuals and foster a spirit of community involvement in reducing crime is referred to as

   A) Community relations activity
   B) Interactional improvement programs
   C) Community volunteer programs
   D) None of the above

The correct answer is A:) Community relations activity.

68) Which federal law enforcement agency was developed through the Volstead Act?

   A) FBI
   B) U.S. Marshals
   C) ICE
   D) DEA

The correct answer is D:) DEA. Although it was not referred to as the DEA, the Volstead Act helped develop what would be called the DEA.

69) Which federal law enforcement agency was originally developed under the IRS?

   A) FBI
   B) U.S. Marshals
   C) ICE
   D) DEA

The correct answer is D:) DEA. The DEA was originally categorized as a miscellaneous division under the IRS.

70) Which federal law enforcement agency is responsible for combating major white-collar crime?

   A) FBI
   B) U.S. Marshals
   C) ICE
   D) DEA

The correct answer is A:) FBI.

71) The State of North Carolina is an example of a:

   A) Centralized state law enforcement organization
   B) Decentralized state law enforcement organization
   C) Laissez-faire state law enforcement organization
   D) None of the above

The correct answer is B:) Decentralized state law enforcement organization. North Carolina has multiple independent law enforcement organizations.

72) Which of the following is NOT a role of the police?

   A) Enforce laws
   B) Keep the peace
   C) Provide services
   D) None of the above

The correct answer is D:) None of the above. All of these are acceptable roles of law enforcement.

73) Which of the following is a benefit to an officer of staying on the police force longer?

   A) More opportunities for promotion with time
   B) Given less dangerous assignments with time
   C) Pay rate increases with experience
   D) Both A and C

The correct answer is D:) Both A and C. Like many jobs, both the available opportunities and the pay increases as an officer gains experience.

74) Which of the following is not included as part of the role of "enforcing laws"?

   A) Investigating offenses
   B) Interrogating suspects
   C) Resolving disputes
   D) Conducting searches

The correct answer is C:) Resolving disputes. Resolving disputes would be considered a service or peacekeeping role.

75) The police's ability to fulfill the role of "peacekeeper" largely depends on what?

   A) Community's acceptance of that role
   B) Officer's individual temperament
   C) Specific departmental policies
   D) None of the above

The correct answer is A:) Community's acceptance of that role. The community must support the police in their attempt to keep the peace in order for them to be successful.

76) Which of the following is not true about the police's role as service provider?

   A) All police embrace this role
   B) It can include such things as giving directions
   C) Some police disagree with having to provide social services
   D) None of the above

The correct answer is A:) All police embrace this role. Some police resent having to provide social services.

77) Which of the following is true about police accreditation through CALEA?

   A) It is funded by grants from the federal government
   B) It allows officers to wear a CALEA badge
   C) It is not mandatory
   D) None of the above

The correct answer is C:) It is not mandatory. CALEA accreditation is completely voluntary.

78) Which of the following is not one of the four kinds of stress found in law enforcement?

   A) External
   B) Personal
   C) Occupational
   D) Organizational

The correct answer is C:) Occupational. The other three along with "operational" are the four types of stress in law enforcement.

79) In the fight against corruption, "managerial solutions" refer to:

   A) Changing the task environment and changing the political environment
   B) Staff turnover, accountability, close supervision of supervisors, and ending corrupted practices
   C) Exposure to criminality, street smarts, lure of money
   D) None of the above

The correct answer is B:) Staff turnover, accountability, close supervision of supervisors, and ending corrupted practices.

80) What is the term that means: the power of choice exercised by law enforcement personnel in the carrying out of their duties?

   A) Free will
   B) Exposure
   C) Discretion
   D) None of the above

The correct answer is C:) Discretion.

81) What determines an officer's use of discretion?

   A) Departmental policy
   B) Officer background
   C) Suspect characteristics
   D) All of the above

The correct answer is D:) All of the above. All of these are factors in police discretion.

82) Which style of policing is characterized by policing "by the book"?

   A) Legalistic
   B) Watchman
   C) Service
   D) Community oriented

The correct answer is A:) Legalistic. The legalistic style of policing is one that is characterized by little discretion and strict adherence to the rules.

83) Which style of policing is characterized by discretion and the use of old fashioned alternatives to arrest?

   A) Legalistic
   B) Watchman
   C) Service
   D) Community oriented

The correct answer is B:) Watchman. The watchman style of policing may resort to strong-arm tactics rather than arrests.

84) Which of the following styles of policing began as an attempt to improve the image of police?

   A) Early police-community interaction
   B) Watchman
   C) Service
   D) Community oriented

The correct answer is A:) Early police-community interaction. While this early style evolved into community policing it was originally motivated by image.

85) Which of the following was not a goal of the Public Safety Partnership and Community Policing act of 1994?

   A) Increase the number of police interacting with the community
   B) Provide additional comprehensive training to officers
   C) Educate the community on drug prevention
   D) Encourage the use of new technology

The correct answer is C:) Educate the community on drug prevention. While this may have been an outcome of some of the community oriented programs, it was not an explicitly stated goal of the act.

86) Where has community policing been the best received?

   A) Wealthy neighborhoods
   B) California
   C) High-crime neighborhoods
   D) None of the above

The correct answer is A:) Wealthy neighborhoods. The reason for this is because the citizens in wealthy neighborhoods already had trust in the police.

87) Which Amendment protects against self-incrimination?

   A) 4th
   B) 5th
   C) 6th
   D) 8th

The correct answer is B:) 5th. The Fifth Amendment protects citizens from incriminating themselves.

88) Which Amendment protects against unreasonable searches and seizures?

   A) 4th
   B) 5th
   C) 6th
   D) 8th

The correct answer is A:) 4th. The Fourth Amendment protects citizens from unreasonable searches and seizures.

89) Which amendment grants citizens the right to counsel?

   A) 4th
   B) 5th
   C) 6th
   D) 8th

The correct answer is C:) 6th. The Sixth Amendment gives citizens the right to an attorney.

90) Which amendment protects citizens from double jeopardy?

   A) 4th
   B) 5th
   C) 6th
   D) 8th

The correct answer is B:) 5th. The Fifth Amendment protects you from double jeopardy.

91) The law of precedence is also referred to as:

   A) Stare divisio
   B) Stare decisis
   C) Law of jurisprudence
   D) None of the above

The correct answer is B:) Stare decisis. Stare decisis translates to "to stand by what is decided."

92) Which Supreme Court case was the basis of the exclusionary rule?

   A) Chimel v. California
   B) Mapp v. Ohio
   C) Weeks v. U.S.
   D) Silverthorne Lumber Co. v. U.S.

The correct answer is C:) Weeks v. U.S. This case laid the groundwork for the exclusionary rule.

93) Which Supreme Court case took what was originally only applied to federal law enforcement and made it applicable to all law enforcement?

   A) Chimel v. California
   B) Mapp v. Ohio
   C) Weeks v. U.S.
   D) Silverthorne Lumber Co. v. U.S.

The correct answer is B:) Mapp v. Ohio. This case brought the exclusionary rule and other decisions to the forefront in law enforcement across the nation.

94) Which evidentiary rule states that evidence derived from illegally seized evidence is not admissible in court?

   A) Exclusionary rule
   B) Fruit of the poisoned tree doctrine
   C) Rule of admissibility
   D) None of the above

The correct answer is B:) Fruit of the poisoned tree doctrine. This was established in the case of Silverthorne Lumber Co. v. U.S.

95) What case established the good faith exception to the exclusionary rule?

   A) U.S. v. Leon
   B) Chimel v. California
   C) Silverthorne Lumber Co. v. U.S.
   D) Harris v. U.S.

The correct answer is A:) U.S. v. Leon. This case was established under the Burgher court.

96) Which Supreme Court era was marked by attention to protection of individual rights as never seen before?

   A) Rehnquist Court
   B) Warren Court
   C) Burgher Court
   D) None of the above

The correct answer is B:) Warren Court. This court under the leadership of Chief Justice Warren made strides in the protection of people accused in the criminal justice system.

97) Which rule was established in the case of Harris v. U.S. (1968)?

   A) Plain view doctrine
   B) Exclusionary rule
   C) Search incident to arrest
   D) None of the above

The correct answer is A:) Plain view doctrine. Harris v. U.S. was decided in 1968 in a case involving the search of an automobile.

98) Which of the following is true when police are searching a vehicle in which consent was granted?

   A) Only areas within reach of the defendant may be searched
   B) The trunk cannot be searched
   C) All areas of the car can be searched
   D) No locked boxes can be opened

The correct answer is C:) All areas of the car can be searched. If someone allows the police to search their vehicle, the police can search any place within the vehicle.

99) Which of the following is NOT one of the three requirements of admissible evidence?

   A) Materiality
   B) Relevancy
   C) Competency
   D) Culpability

The correct answer is D:) Culpability. Materiality, relevancy and competency are the three requirements.

100) Which of the following is true about the plain view doctrine?

   A) It allows for an officer to look under objects that are in plain view
   B) It was established through Mapp v. Ohio
   C) It only applies to searches incident to arrest
   D) It was established through Harris v. U.S.

The correct answer is D:) It was established through Harris v. U.S. The plain view doctrine does not allow officers to look under or move anything out of the way.

101) Which of the following is NOT a reason for an emergency search without a warrant?

A) Public safety
B) Potential escape of a dangerous suspect
C) Potential for theft of property
D) Destruction of evidence

The correct answer is C:) Potential for theft of property. The others do qualify a situation as an emergency.

102) What is the accepted standard when determining if an arrest has been made?

A) If the Miranda rights have been read
B) "Freedom to leave"
C) Presence of handcuffs
D) None of the above

The correct answer is B:) "Freedom to leave." If a person is free to leave the situation, an arrest has not taken place.

103) What case decided the "stop and frisk" right of police?

A) Chimel v. California
B) Terry v. Ohio
C) Robinson v. Ohio
D) Brown v. Mississippi

The correct answer is B:) Terry v. Ohio. The stop and frisk is also known as a "terry stop."

104) Which case clarified that physical abuse was not an acceptable form of interrogation?

A) Brown v. Mississippi
B) Ashcraft v. Tennessee
C) Minnick v. Mississippi
D) None of the above

The correct answer is A:) Brown v. Mississippi. This decision came after the state of Mississippi originally upheld the decision.

105) What group numbered over 100 men in Charleston S.C. in 1937, making it the largest "law enforcement" group in the country?

   A) Burgher guard
   B) Rattle watch
   C) Slave patrol
   D) None of the above

The correct answer is C:) Slave patrol. This group of men primarily tracked escaped slaves.

106) Which term refers to the theory that the most powerful people should be above the law?

   A) Spoils system
   B) Hierarchy of lawlessness
   C) Survival of the fittest
   D) Victor reward system

The correct answer is A:) Spoils system. This system states "to the victor goes the spoils."

107) Which of the following does not have a U.S. federal district court?

   A) Guam
   B) Northern Marina Islands
   C) Virgin Islands
   D) None of the above

The correct answer is D:) None of the above. All of these areas have a district court.

108) In which of the following situations would the evidence described be inadmissible?

   A) Financial records of the head of a corporation involved in tax fraud.
   B) Evidence which was collected before a search warrant was obtained.
   C) Maps of the crime scene.
   D) Both A and B

The correct answer is B:) Evidence which was collected before a search warrant was obtained. This evidence would have been collected illegally and would not be admissible in court.

109) Which of the following goals of corrections is related to the term *lex talionis*?

   A) Incapacitation
   B) Retribution
   C) Deterrence
   D) Rehabilitation

The correct answer is B:) Retribution. *Lex talionis* is the concept of "an eye for an eye."

110) Which of the following goals of corrections is related to the concept of "medical model"?

   A) Incapacitation
   B) Retribution
   C) Deterrence
   D) Rehabilitation

The correct answer is D:) Rehabilitation. The medical model thought of all criminals as ill and in need of rehabilitation.

111) What is the term used to describe a situation where a judge releases a suspect on a promise to return?

   A) Bail
   B) Recognizance
   C) Remittance
   D) None of the above

The correct answer is B:) Recognizance. When a judge releases someone on their own recognizance there is no exchange of money, just a promise to return for future court dates.

112) What was the first federal law enforcement agency to be created?

   A) FBI
   B) I.C.E. (formerly I.N.S.)
   C) U.S. Marshals
   D) None of the above

The correct answer is C:) U.S. Marshals. The U.S. Marshals were created by George Washington in 1789.

113) What was the first state to have an organized state run law enforcement agency?

   A) Maryland
   B) Texas
   C) North Carolina
   D) New York

The correct answer is B:) Texas. The Texas Rangers were the first state-run police force.

114) What types of tests are typically required for police applicants?

   A) Psychological
   B) Intelligence
   C) Physical
   D) All of the above

The correct answer is D:) All of the above. These tests became commonplace with the professionalization of the police.

115) Writing reports and time management are examples of what kind of stressors?

   A) Organizational
   B) Personal
   C) Official
   D) External

The correct answer is A:) Organizational. Organizational stress is that which is brought on by staying organized, managing paperwork and time.

116) What is the term used to describe the difficulty in finding a concrete definition of "corruption"?

   A) Thin blue line
   B) Blue code
   C) Slippery slope
   D) None of the above

The correct answer is C:) Slippery slope. Because there is a large grey area in what is considered corruption, a slippery slope defines it well.

117) Why can't officers who test positive for drugs be immediately fired?

   A) It would be unethical
   B) It is a disease protected by law
   C) Departments don't mind casual drug use by police
   D) Precedence doesn't allow it

The correct answer is B:) It is a disease protected by law. Because of this departments will attempt to get help for officers with a drug problem.

118) An individual's right to protection against unreasonable search and seizure is an example of what?

   A) A right not guaranteed in the Constitution but through precedence
   B) Procedural due process right
   C) Substantive due process right
   D) None of the above

The correct answer is B:) Procedural due process right. This right is guaranteed by the 4th Amendment.

119) Which of the following was developed in the case of Chimel v. California (1969)?

   A) Due process
   B) Search incident to arrest
   C) Stop and frisk
   D) None of the above

The correct answer is B:) Search incident to arrest. This case defined what areas could be searched when making an arrest, without a search warrant.

120) What is the standard used when determining if an area has protection from unreasonable search and seizure?

   A) Castle doctrine
   B) Plain view
   C) Reasonable expectation of privacy
   D) None of the above

The correct answer is C:) Reasonable expectation of privacy. If a person has a reasonable expectation surrounding an area, then that area is most likely protected under the 4th Amendment.

121) Which of the following must be present for someone to waive their Miranda rights?

   A) Knowledge of the rights
   B) Understanding of the rights
   C) Knowledge of the consequences of the waiver
   D) All of the above

The correct answer is D:) All of the above.

122) Which of the following are individuals not protected from at interrogations?

   A) Abuse
   B) Coercion
   C) Self coercion
   D) None of the above

The correct answer is C:) Self coercion. Self coercion is not something that law enforcement can be responsible for.

123) Which case involved the weekend long interrogation of a suspect and resulted in coercion not being allowed as an interrogation technique?

   A) Terry v. Ohio
   B) Brown v. Mississippi
   C) Ashcraft v. Tennessee
   D) None of the above

The correct answer is C:) Ashcraft v. Tennessee. This case established coercion as an interrogation technique that would not hold up in court.

124) Which of the following cases determined that a person does not have to identify themselves to the police if there is not probable cause present for the officer to request that information?

   A) Brown v. Mississippi
   B) Brown v. Texas
   C) Smith v. Ohio
   D) None of the above

The correct answer is B:) Brown v. Texas. This case involved the police questioning someone because they were curious.

125) What is the purpose of a stop and frisk?

    A) To uncover illegal substances
    B) To ensure officer safety
    C) To perform a search incident to arrest
    D) None of the above

The correct answer is B:) To ensure officer safety. Officer's are only looking for weapons in a stop and frisk.

126) Which of the following is a true concern of police administration?

    A) Officer mental health
    B) Community involvement
    C) Proper funding
    D) All of the above

The correct answer is D:) All of the above. Police administration has many concerns and has to balance all of them in an effort to address the most important.

Test-Taking Strategies

Here are some test-taking strategies that are specific to this test and to other DSST tests in general:

- Keep your eyes on the time. Pay attention to how much time you have left.
- Read the entire question and read all the answers. Many questions are not as hard to answer as they may seem. Sometimes, a difficult sounding question really only is asking you how to read an accompanying chart. Chart and graph questions are on most DANTES/DSST tests and should be an easy free point.
- If you don't know the answer immediately, the new computer-based testing lets you mark questions and come back to them later if you have time.
- Read the wording carefully. Some words can give you hints to the right answer. There are no exceptions to an answer when there are words in the question such as always, all or none. If one of the answer choices includes most or some of the right answers, but not all, then that is not the answer. Here is an example:

   The primary colors include all of the following:
   - A) Red, Yellow, Blue, Green
   - B) Red, Green, Yellow
   - C) Red, Orange, Yellow
   - D) Red, Yellow, Blue

   Although item A includes all the right answers, it also includes an incorrect answer, making it incorrect. If you didn't read it carefully, were in a hurry, or didn't know the material well, you might fall for this.

- Make a guess on a question that you do not know the answer to. There is no penalty for an incorrect answer. Eliminate the answer choices that you know are incorrect. For example, this will let your guess be a 1 in 3 chance instead.

Test Preparation

How much you need to study depends on your knowledge of a subject area. If you are interested in literature, took it in school, or enjoy reading then your study and preparation for the literature or humanities test will not need to be as intensive as that of someone who is new to literature.

This book is much different than the regular DANTES/DSST study guides. This book actually teaches you the information that you need to know to pass the test. If you are particularly interested in an area, or feel that you want more information, do a quick search online. We've tried not to include too much depth in areas that are not as essential on the test. Everything in this book will be on the test. It is important to understand all major theories and concepts listed in the table of contents. It is also important to know any bolded words.

Don't worry if you do not understand or know a lot about the area. With minimal study, you can complete and pass the test.

One of the fallacies of other test books is test questions. People assume that the content of the questions are similar to what will be on the test. That is not the case. They are only there to test your "test taking skills" so for those who know to read a question carefully, there is not much added value from taking a "fake" test.

To prepare for the test, make a series of goals. Allot a certain amount of time to review the information you have already studied and to learn additional material. Take notes as you study; it will help you learn the material.

Legal Note

All rights reserved. This Study Guide, Book and Flashcards are protected under the U.S. Copyright Law. No part of this book or study guide or flashcards may be reproduced, distributed or stored in a retrieval system, or transmitted in any form or by any means, electronic, mechanical, photocopying, recording, or otherwise, without the prior written permission of the publisher Breely Crush Publishing LLC.

FLASHCARDS

This section contains flashcards for you to use to further your understanding of the material and test yourself on important concepts, names or dates. Read the term or question then flip the page over to check the answer on the back. Keep in mind that this information may not be covered in the text of the study guide. Take your time to study the flashcards, you will need to know and understand these concepts to pass the test.

Miranda v. Arizona	**Escobedo v. Illinois**
Ashcraft v. Tennessee	**Smith v. Ohio**
Terry v. Ohio	**Maryland v. Buie**
South Dakota v. Opperman	**stare decisis**

Failure to recognize Escobedo's constitutional right to counsel	Right to remain silent, that anything he says can be used against him in court, that he has a right to an attorney and if he can't afford one he will be appointed one
A right to protect their property from unsubstantiated police search	This case established that "inherent coercion" could also bring about a false confession and therefore was not allowed
Which allowed for the searching of premises where a dangerous person may be hiding	Guaranteed an officer's right to "stop and frisk" individuals when they are ensuring their safety
Precedence	That the police could search a vehicle for the purposes of inventorying property while it was impounded

Substantive due process	**4th Amendment**
5th Amendment	**Protection from doublejeopardy**
Right to a speedy trial	**Right to reasonable bail**
Organizational stress	**Frankpledge system**

To be free from unreasonable searches and seizures	The creation and definition of what a person's rights are
5th Amendment	Protection against selfincrimination
8th Amendment	6th Amendment
It required that all men pledge peace to the King	Completing paperwork, scheduling training, writing reports add to organizational stress

Thief takers	The London Metropolitan Police Force was founded by who?
Pendleton Act	August Vollmer
Orlando Wilson	Kerner Commission
General jurisdiction	Circuit

Sir Robert Peel	Captured criminals and returned stolen goods to victims of theft who offered the right reward
Father of modern law enforcement	An attempt to reduce corruption
Addressed issues such as police brutality, riots, and discrimination	Streamlined hiring and training practices within the Chicago department
A group of federal districts	Can hear all cases, regardless of class or severity

| Deterrence | Rehabilitation |

| Retribution | Auburn system |

| Pennsylvania system | Parole |

| Recognizance | Continuance |

Goal that focuses on changing the offender through sentencing	To preventing future crime from being committed
Subjected to hard labor every day and silence was enforced	Criminals need to pay for their actions and sees corrections as solely a system of punishment
Early, supervised release from prison	Requiring absolute solitude while allowed to read only the Bible
A delay or extension	Just a promise to return and is similar to bail in that regard, but no money or collateral is put up

Plea bargain	NCVS
UCR	Clearance rate
NIBRS	How many U.S. Marshals are there?
DEA	Weeks v. U.S.

National Crime Victimization Survey	When the defendant agrees to plead guilty to a lesser charge
Crime that is resolved with an arrest	Uniform Crime Report
94	National Incident-Based Reporting
Formed the basis of the exclusionary rule	Drug Enforcement Agency

Exclusionary rule	Silverthorne Lumber Co. v. U.S.
Fruit of the poisoned tree	Mapp v. Ohio
Good faith exception to the exclusionary rule	Maryland v. Garrison
Illinois v. Rodriguez	Plain view doctrine

Resulted in fruit of the poisoned tree	Incriminating evidence must be seized in accordance with the constitutional elements of due process
This case established fruit of the poisoned tree to all law enforcement throughout the country (not just federal)	Like illegally seized evidence is not admissible in court, neither is evidence derived from illegally seized evidence
Evidence was admissible even if the information on the warrant was incorrect	U.S. v. Leon
Harris v. U.S.	If the police had a reasonable belief that a person had the right to consent to a search, they could legally search

NOTES

NOTES

NOTES

NOTES

NOTES

NOTES

NOTES

NOTES

NOTES

NOTES